SHARLY

MANAGER ONBOARDING

5 Steps for Setting New Leaders Up for Success

SHARLYN LAUBY

MANAGER ONBOARDING

5 Steps for Setting New Leaders Up for Success

Society for Human Resource Management
Alexandria, VA | **shrm.org**

Society for Human Resource Management, India Office
Mumbai, India | **shrmindia.org**

Society for Human Resource Management
Haidian District Beijing, China | **shrm.org/cn**

**Society for Human Resource Management,
Middle East and Africa Office**
Dubai, UAE | **shrm.org/pages/mena.aspx**

The Society for Human Resource Management (SHRM) is the world's largest HR professional society, representing 285,000 members in more than 165 countries. For nearly seven decades, the Society has been the leading provider of resources serving the needs of HR professionals and advancing the practice of human resource management. SHRM has more than 575 affiliated chapters within the United States and subsidiary offices in China, India and United Arab Emirates. Visit us at shrm.org.

Interior and Cover Design: Terry Biddle, Shirley E.M. Raybuck

Library of Congress Cataloging-in-Publication Data

(on file)

16-0225

Contents

Dedication

A book never happens alone.
As a consultant, I've always said that I work with terrific people and
companies on fun, engaging projects. This one is no exception.
My thanks to Christopher Anzalone and the entire SHRM team for
giving me this opportunity. It has been fabulous working with you
on this project. Your guidance and suggestions have helped shaped
the human resources conversation about manager onboarding.
A huge thanks to all of the people and organizations who
shared their onboarding best practices and lessons learned. You
didn't have to, but we are all glad you did. You're leading the
way for better manager onboarding programs to exist.
Lastly, all my love and admiration to my husband, Keith, who
still listens to my crazy ideas. I'm one very lucky girl.
Thank you all and enjoy the read. Cheers!

—Sharlyn Lauby

Preface

Onboarding is such an important part of an employee's success. It starts well before the employee decides to apply with an organization in the forms of employment branding and the candidate experience. It includes sourcing, interviewing, background checks, and extending the job offer. Next comes new-hire paperwork, orientation, and training. Lastly, performance management. On some level much of onboarding touches every single component in the employee life cycle.

Yet, when it comes to onboarding managers, we do nothing or very little.

But we expect managers to help onboard new employees. They are an active part of the recruiting process. Managers are expected to train and develop employees. They are required to coach and mentor employees for exceptional performance.

It's time for organizations to give managers the same foundation for success that we give new-hire employees.

In 2015, I had this conversation with Christopher Anzalone at the Society for Human Resource Management (SHRM) Annual Conference & Exposition. He mentioned to me that manager onboarding was a frequently requested topic in the SHRM Knowledge Center. My immediate response was "Yes!" I can see why this would be a widely requested topic. What amazed me was that no one was really talking about it. So I decided to take on the challenge.

This book will walk you through the process of creating a manager onboarding program. While onboarding has many touchpoints in a manager's career, this book is going to focus on the new-hire or newly promoted phase. We're going to focus on the part of the process that hasn't been created. The part that desperately *needs* to be created.

Companies haven't stopped hiring people. There are many great books out there about branding, strategy, sourcing, and hiring. There are also dozens of books about training and performance management. This book will help you set the manager you've just hired or promoted up for success.

And in my humble opinion, this couldn't come at a better time.

Job seekers are doing their homework before they apply with an organization. Research from Glassdoor showed that 62 percent of job seekers are influenced by employee reviews.[1] Those reviews include corporate culture, management practices, and the work environment. Candidates are making judgement calls about your organization long before they apply.

A poor candidate experience is costing companies. A survey from Recruiting Daily revealed that 47 percent of candidates have no previous relationship with a company before applying for a job.[2] This means the candidate experience is the first impression of a company. Couple that with 11 percent of respondents saying their candidate experience was bad enough to sever all ties with the company (as a candidate and a customer), and it's worth paying attention to.

Employee engagement is stagnant. Gallup reported that employee engagement in the U.S. was stagnant in 2015 at 32 percent.[3] Yes, three out of five employees are not engaged. I know we toss around the term "employee engagement" a lot, but the truth is . . . engagement matters to the bottom line.

Who touches all of these processes? That's right. Managers.

So it makes absolutely no sense to simply promote or hire someone into a manager position and not give him or her the tools for success.

I wrote this book for human resource and business professionals who are looking for a roadmap to designing a manager onboarding program. My goal was to share just a bit of theory and a whole lot of practical knowledge. I also reached out to my friends, colleagues, and clients for stories and examples about how their onboarding programs work—both for new employees as well as for managers. We don't have to recreate the wheel, and you can use their best practices as inspiration for your own.

While at a 2015 conference in London, I heard many HR executives talk about the need to invest in managers. I believe onboarding is the place to start. Let managers know on day one that you're invested in their success because you need for *them* to be engaged too. I've never seen a disengaged manager engage his or her team members and coach them to high performance.

Here's how we're going to tackle the project. The book is divided into six parts.

In **Part I, Manager Onboarding Defined**, I've broken down the definitions so we're on the same page. You might need this when it comes to explaining and selling the program to senior management.

Part II, The Business Case for Manager Onboarding, offers some thoughts on how to sell the program to senior management and acquire the resources (that is, head count and budget) necessary for the project.

In **Part III**, I outline the **5 Steps to Developing a Manager Onboarding Program** using a common instructional design model. This will help organize the program content.

What program content, you say? Well, **Part IV, Manager Onboarding Content** provides some insight into the different topics to consider for manager onboarding (versus your leadership development program).

Part V, Post-Onboarding Strategies suggests some activities that can be used after the formal onboarding process is completed, so the learning continues.

And finally, **Part VI, Measuring Program Effectiveness** gives some tips for showing the metrics and numbers behind the program. We'll also address program maintenance.

You can read the book like a reference guide, using each section as you need it. Or you can read the book cover to cover for putting together a project plan. I can also see several members of the project design team referencing the book.

I hope you find the book helpful in your journey to creating a manager onboarding program. It's been a delight writing it. My thanks to my family, friends, colleagues, clients, and the team at SHRM for supporting me through the process. Now, let's build a practical and effective manager onboarding program, shall we?

Part I:

Manager Onboarding Defined

"The true measure of the value of any business leader and manager is performance."

—*Brian Tracy*

Chapter 1.

What Is a Manager?

Let me start with a simple request. Please do not read the title of this chapter and decide this book isn't worth your time. I realize there are whole books devoted to the study of management.

This is not one of them.

This book is a practical guide to help organizations create an onboarding process that will help employees become productive in their new role as a manager. That being said, it's necessary to talk about the definition of management because it frames the conversation.

Whenever I want to talk about a definition, I find it helpful to do what I did in school and reach for a dictionary. In the technology age, of course, that means doing a Google search. If you search for the definition of management, it says "the process of dealing with or controlling things or people." Since organizations are composed of things and people, it's no surprise that the Oxford Dictionaries definition of a manager is "a person responsible for controlling or administering all or part of a company or similar organization."

So for this book, the word "manager" will focus on those responsibilities commonly identified with management: planning, staffing, organizing, coordinating, and controlling.

"Planning" is the process of establishing a goal and creating a course of action to achieve that goal.

"Staffing" involves hiring the right people to achieve the goals of the organization.

"Organizing" includes developing an organizational structure and designating tasks to employees.

"Coordinating" consists of the communication, direction, and feedback necessary to make sure the organization meets its goals.

"Controlling" includes adding performance standards and monitoring employee results.

Now that we've defined what management is and what managers do, let's also address the one other quality often associated with being a manager: leadership.

Managers versus Leaders

A conversation about managers and management always seems to prompt a conversation about leaders and leadership. Frankly, I'm surprised when I read articles comparing management and leadership. I don't understand the comparison. In my mind, they are two completely different things. It's like comparing apples and pianos.

We've already talked about the definition of a manager. Let's do the same with the word "leader." The *Free Dictionary* defines a leader as "one who has influence or power." Using this definition of leadership tells us a couple of things:

1. Leaders exist at every level of an organization. They may or may not also be managers.
2. If you're a manager, you have some leadership power by virtue of your position.

If we want to cultivate leadership within our organizations, we have to recognize that leadership exists in everyone. It's about understanding how an individual's leadership manifests itself in actions and behaviors. It's about using our leadership ability in the right way and at the right times. Companies need leaders beyond the ones holding a manager job title. And individuals holding a manager job title need to realize that their boss, co-workers, and team members all have leadership ability. This will change the way they view their role.

In your organization, you may or may not use the terms leader and manager interchangeably. Again, the reason I'm defining leaders and managers is because this book is not about comparing and contrasting leadership and management. That might imply a zero-sum game. That is, great managers aren't great leaders, and vice versa. For this book, we will consider leaders and managers to perform two different roles in the organization. Companies need both of them to be successful.

Here's another way to look at it. Several months ago, I had the opportunity to interview Ken Blanchard, Ph.D., author of the best-selling book *The One Minute Manager*,[1] for my blog, *HR Bartender*, and I asked him about the difference between management and leadership.[2] He said, "I never like to get in an argument about leadership and management, because whenever they are compared, management takes second fiddle, due to the fact that leadership sounds so much more exciting. Yet there are really two parts of leadership."

Blanchard explained the two parts of leadership. "The first is *strategic leadership*—which involves vision and direction—the second is *operational leadership*, which involves implementing the vision. The part that entails setting the vision and direction is what people usually associate with leadership. The part that entails implementation—how you accomplish the goals and live according to the vision—is thought of as management. But I really think both are aspects of leadership."

Leadership is a part of management. But it's not the only part of management. Excellent leadership skills are needed at every level of the organization. We will address leadership in this book along with the functions of management.

People versus Process Managers

Another manager comparison that happens quite frequently is the "people" versus "process" manager, the definitions being that people managers have direct reports and process managers do not. Sometimes a judgment is made that people managers are more valuable because of their responsibility to manage their direct reports. Let's put that comment to rest right now. All managers deal with people and process, regardless of direct reports. Human resources is a great example:

- A recruiting manager has a team of recruiting staff. The recruiting manager manages people, but he or she also manages the recruiting process.
- A recruiting manager without a team manages the recruiting process, but he or she also works with other people.

In fact, some might argue that the solo recruiting manager has a tougher job managing the process by working with the hiring managers, payroll, and other functions than the recruiting manager with a team. My point is this: The goal of this book isn't to debate whether people or process is better, tougher, or more valuable. The point is, people and process are intertwined. Even individual contributors with a manager title do not operate in a silo.

Another reason that the people-versus-process distinction isn't necessary is due to the increasing number of times a manager is placed in charge of a project team or task force. A common example might be the technology manager who is responsible for a project implementation team to roll out a new software solution. The technology manager could be a process manager and, because of his or her extensive knowledge about the process, the manager is placed in charge of the implementation. It's critical for project success that the technology manager knows how to manage his or her team, even if it's a temporary situation.

Bottom line: If you're a manager, you have to deal with both people and process. And you have to learn how to deal with both successfully.

Manager Career Lifecycles

I recently heard someone say, "There's no such thing as a career ladder. It's more of a career obstacle course." While the image is humorous to envision, the comment offers a good perspective. Many of us are not doing the jobs we thought we would after leaving school. That doesn't mean we're unhappy or disengaged. It does mean that as we spend more time in the working world, our role as a manager evolves. So in having a conversation about manager onboarding, we need to consider the needs of both employees and managers at every phase of their careers.

A perfect example is happening right now in today's workforce. As the Baby Boomer generation is planning its exit from the workforce, Millennials are establishing their early careers. Millennial managers need to be ready to manage their own career needs as well as support the career needs of their Baby Boomer workforce.

Millennial Managers Are the New Face of Business

According to the "Multi-Generational Leadership Study"[3] conducted by Workplace, an executive development firm, and Beyond, an employment site, a growing number of Millennials (83 percent) are managing Generation X and Baby Boomer professionals. However, 45 percent of Baby Boomers and Generation X respondents felt that Millennials' lack of managerial experience could have a negative impact on the organizational culture. On a related note, over one-third of Millennial respondents indicated that it's difficult to manage older generations.

"Millennials are no longer new to the workforce, they're now in the thick of it," said Rich Milgram, founder and CEO of Beyond. "However, a significant portion of the older employees they're managing don't have faith in their abilities. The only way to overcome this unique challenge is through a range of professional learning and development delivery options, including formal training, mentoring, coaching, and online self-directed learning. This will help create a culture of learning that benefits all generations, and provides employees with the tools and resources they need to flourish as leaders."

In the book *Defining HR Success*, the authors talked about different professional career levels such as early, mid, and senior/executive (I like to call it "late career").[4] Within these career levels, we travel a progression of sorts starting with our first jobs. Our needs and the company's expectations for us differ during each phase.

Early Career: Establishing Your Long-Term Goals

The early-career phase can involve a couple of dimensions. First, it can be the time when employees have their first few jobs and are learning those skills that make them great employees. Examples might be working with occupational schedules, dress codes, and company policies and procedures. The second aspect can be when employees are trying to find their chosen professions. It might be the jobs we held while we were getting our education.

Those first impressions of the working world are incredibly important, and they shape how we view management. Our first managers might have more influence than they realize on our decision to become a manager in the future. And this is crucial when it comes to the role of a manager and his or her ultimate success.

Midcareer: Dedication to Your Profession

During the midcareer phase, employees are considered generalists or specialists in their chosen fields. They manage programs, processes, and people. And they can hold a formal title within the organization, such as manager or director. (Note: When we discuss manager onboarding in this book, we could also be talking about supervisors, directors, vice presidents, and other roles. It's about what the position does, not what the position is called.)

Also during midcareer, employees are looking to refine their knowledge and skills. It's possible they will explore opportunities outside of their departments or organizations. Managers need to be confident and trust that employees will make the right decisions about their careers. Their responsibility is to play the role of coach.

Late Career: Sharing Your Knowledge and Expertise

In the late-career phase, we are considered very experienced in our profession. We may or may not be an executive. We also may or may not have tenure with one organization. Also, during this stage, we might be formally or informally considering semi-retirement or some sort of planned exit strategy. (Note: Career stages aren't driven by age. There are many people who have multiple careers in their lifetime.)

Later in our careers, the focus changes from developing ourselves to developing others. Hopefully, we've had a fortunate career and want to pass along what we've learned. The organization wants that as well.

It wants experienced managers to share their knowledge with high-potential employees.

Which leads me to the most important role that managers have . . .

Managers Have One Job

. . . and that's to identify and groom their replacements.

If managers take their jobs seriously, then part of their function is staffing. Not just staffing their team but thinking about who will replace them. For the organization to run well, managers must be able to take a day off, leave the office for training, and go on vacation without the department falling apart. If the company is going to be able to meet its short- and long-term goals, managers must think beyond the here and now.

That's why managers need onboarding that is specific to their role. We are giving managers a role and, at the same time, asking them to prepare for giving it away. Organizations need to set managers up for success.

Managers need to realize that the role of being a manager isn't to be indispensable. They must be willing to share control, power, and authority with employees. In addition, they need to be able to delegate comfortably and effectively.

Ultimately, organizations want managers who are constantly thinking about talent. They want the managers' job of finding and training their replacements to permeate the organization. That takes more than a management development program. In the next chapter, we'll dissect onboarding and discuss why it's the appropriate method for new managers to quickly become productive.

Chapter 2.

What Is Onboarding?

Years ago, onboarding was synonymous with orientation. Today, onboarding has transformed into a process that's much longer and broader in scope. Some organizations have given onboarding a different name to breathe new life into an old concept. For example, at NCR onboarding is called First Steps to represent your first steps with the organization. The program was created by Wendy Smith, the leader of new employee experiences at NCR.[1] Again, "new employee experiences" is a fresh new phrase.

The reason I'm bringing this up is because it's not about what you call the program. For this book, we're going to call it onboarding. It includes several different phases and activities. The goal of onboarding hasn't changed.

> Onboarding is a process that helps employees become productive in the most effective and efficient means possible.

While it's hard to track the history of onboarding, the term seems to date back to the 1970s when it was introduced as "organizational socialization," which is defined as the process through which employees learn the knowledge, skills, and behaviors to become effective. It included meetings, trainings, and printed materials. Organizational socialization leads to positive outcomes such as higher job satisfaction, better performance, and reduced stress.

But the primary reason onboarding was created is quite clear: *turnover is expensive.* An article in *Fast Company* stated that 31 percent of new employees quit a job within the first six months.[2] Organizations cannot achieve their goals and objectives if they don't have employees. Managers can't accomplish their goals if they are constantly recruiting. So setting employees up for success (that is, onboarding) is essential for managers and the business.

Organizations realize the importance of onboarding. According to the Sierra-Cedar 2015-2016 HR Systems Survey White Paper, over 40 percent of survey participants plan to work on iniatives to improve recruiting and onboarding business processes.[3] Many of those business plan improvements are in the form of onboarding solutions. Survey responses indicated a 90 percent increase in mobile adoption from the year prior, and another 65 percent increase is forecasted for next year. It's obvious that onboarding is a priority and that finding effective onboarding strategies is key.

Onboarding involves several phases and various activities. I want to spend some time talking about what's involved with onboarding so when we start discussing how to design a manager onboarding program, we're on the same page. If onboarding is the process that helps employees become productive, then it only makes sense that onboarding includes recruiting, orientation, training, performance management, and employee engagement.

Recruiting

We all know recruiting as the process of bringing a person into the organization. It includes employer branding, career portals, sourcing, interviews, selection, and, finally, extending the offer. In the context of manager onboarding, we could be talking about external hires or internal promotions and transfers. Either way, the process is similar.

For external hires, we want managers to be interested in our organization and excited to apply (employer branding). Organizations need a clearly defined and efficient way for applicants to submit their interest (career portals). Recruiters want to identify the most qualified candidates (sourcing), connect them with the department (interviews), choose the best talent (selection), and finally, extend the offer.

Internally, organizations want management candidates who are interested in positions of greater responsibility. An internal job posting process makes it easy for employees to express interest in job openings. The internal recruiting process still needs to source the most qualified candidates, conduct interviews with the department, and select the best person before extending the offer.

> ### Marriott Wandernaut Show
>
> Marriott has been experimenting with different kinds of content to engage not only its associates but job seekers as well. It launched a podcast called *The Wandernaut Show*, which is available on iTunes and SoundCloud. The first five episodes are a conversation with David Rodriguez, Marriott's global chief human resources officer (CHRO).
>
> There are a few things I love about this. First, Marriott is taking advantage of technology to get its message out there. The podcast format is very popular and easy to implement. Secondly, it's great to see the CHRO of a *Fortune* 500 brand putting himself out there in a podcast. And lastly, the goal of the content is to engage both job seekers *and* employees.
>
> As the recruiting market gets tougher, organizations will want to find solutions that check off more than one box. Podcasts like this one from Marriott that can engage and inform both employees and candidates offer a real win-win.

Orientation

Over the years, orientation has gotten a bad rap as it morphed into a half-day paperwork signing event. That's not what orientation was designed to be. Orientation was designed to familiarize a new employee with the company and his or her department.

Some organizations, in an effort to change the perception of orientation, have renamed the paperwork portion of orientation as "preboarding." The goal of preboarding is to get all of the employees' necessary administration and paperwork out of the way so they can focus on their jobs and on building positive working relationships with their manager and co-workers.

Preboarding has been especially helpful for technology providers. Organizations can implement technology solutions that will take care of the administration in an effective and efficient manner. Preboarding provides consistency, which is good for compliance, and it can be scalable.

Onboarding Technology Can Be Used for More Than Onboarding

If you're having trouble selling your organization on an onboarding technology solution, keep in mind that most of these solutions do more than onboarding, even if that's what they're called. We're not going into a deep dive of the details in this book. But when researching an onboarding solution, ask your vendor about handling internships, work events such as transfers and promotions, contingent workers, and offboarding. The technology's ability to track more than onboarding might be the extra value you need to justify the expense.

We have a tendency to think of orientation in a new-hire context. That is, new hires attend orientation. But what about employees who transfer to other departments? Or as in the case of this book—new managers? Orientation should not happen only once in an employee's career. Companies change all the time. Departments change too. More importantly, we cannot make assumptions that new managers know everything there is to know about their new role just because they already work for the company.

O.C. Tanner, a global leader in helping organizations inspire and appreciate great work, uses the term "inboarding" as the process of helping current employees acquire the knowledge, skills, and training they need to be productive.[4] It's possible that the process looks different for managers being hired from the outside than for employees promoted internally. For the purposes of this book, we're going to talk about onboarding in the context of both. There's a benefit to bringing these two groups together in manager onboarding.

Managers need to have peers who can support them. Let's face it, sometimes being a manager is a lonely job. We can't be friends with our employees. Friendly = yes. Friends = gets complicated, especially if a manager has to deliver an unpleasant conversation. So new managers need peers they can talk to.

Managers do not want to seek all of their answers from human resources and their boss. This isn't to say that managers dislike interacting with HR and senior management. But they should be able to find answers to everyday questions from other managers.

When managers hired from the outside and managers promoted from within start collaborating, great things can happen. The organization should encourage the creativity and idea sharing. Everyone can benefit.

Lastly, some employees who have been promoted from within might feel that they know internal processes and that sitting through an onboarding program again would be a waste of their time. It's possible, however, that what they know isn't the proper way to do something. Or it's the old way of doing it. Participating in the onboarding process serves as confirmation that new managers know the correct way to accomplish things.

Training and Development

Training is focused on the skills in your current job. Development gives you the skills for future jobs. Originally, I was only going to mention training in this segment, but at the point people become managers, they need to start focusing on grooming their replacements. This means managers need both training and development at the same time.

One of the worst things companies can do is hire or promote the most technically competent employees to management and then not give them the tools they need to do their jobs. We're going to talk specifically about what those tools are in later chapters, but for now we need to acknowledge that training and development have significant roles in onboarding.

In some organizations, training might be a part of orientation. And that's fine. What's important to realize is what training means. For instance,

- Telling someone the history of the company is not training.
- Explaining the procedure for answering the telephone isn't training.
- Handing out a binder with the emergency evacuation plan is not training.

Training involves more than simply telling someone how to do something. It involves giving the person the ability to practice and learn.

The Difference between Knowledge, Skills, and Abilities

The words knowledge, skills, and abilities (aka KSAs) are often used interchangeably, but they're three different things. It's important to know the difference—even though the difference can be subtle—especially when you're designing an onboarding program.

Knowledge is the theoretical or practical understanding of a subject. For example, an employee might have knowledge of the ADDIE model used in instructional design. This doesn't mean the employee knows how to be an instructional designer. It means he or she knows the model.

Skills are the proficiencies developed through training or experience. Using the ADDIE example, the employee has demonstrated skills in applying the ADDIE model when designing training programs. Skills are usually something that has been learned. So we can develop our skills through the transfer of knowledge.

Abilities are the qualities of being able to do something. There is a fine line between skills and abilities. Most people would say the differentiator is whether the thing in question was learned or is innate. I think of organization and prioritization as abilities that can help an employee develop his or her instructional design skills.

The reason we sometimes use the terms interchangeably is because they are all "must-haves" in our careers. Recruiters look for knowledge, skills, and abilities during the hiring process. Managers use KSAs when they are considering employees for transfers and promotions. Moreover, KSAs are used as companies create and update their replacement and succession plans.

As we talk about skills gaps and onboarding programs, it will be crucial to understand the difference because the way we obtain knowledge, skills, and abilities can vary. And if we're at an organization trying to figure out how to solve skills gaps that exist within our workforce, then we have to link the right solutions.

For instance, if the issue is knowledge, then maybe we can create an in-house library that employees can use to check out books on the topics. But if the challenge is skills, the answer might be training. And if abilities need to be improved, is it possible to develop personal action plans that give employees the opportunity to refine their abilities?

You'll find that, as you are developing your manager onboarding program, there will be times when it's fine to use the terms interchangeably and others when we need to emphasize the exact term. Regardless, they're all equally important.

Performance Management

The whole reason we hire the best employees, tell them about the organization, and give them training is to attain the highest level of performance from them.

High-performing employees = high-performing companies.

That translates into bottom-line results.

Now let's factor in managers. When people become managers, they have a unique role in the performance management process:

1. *They are still employees.* Becoming a manager doesn't mean that we don't have a boss anymore. We still have someone who manages us and ultimately gives us our performance review (based on our new role as a manager).

2. *They are part of a team.* Managers are often tasked with making goals happen with and through their working relationships. On a basic level, managers can secure resources and information by having good working relationships with their peers.

3. *They lead a group or process.* This is likely the reason that they have the title of manager. They've been asked to manage or be responsible for a group or process. Maybe because of their KSAs. Or a combination of these factors.

Chances are when managers are asked what they do for a living, the replies align with number 3 above. "Jose is in charge of supply chain management" or "Leonard manages the marketing department." But the way they receive their pay increases is by virtue of number 1. And the way they accomplish their goals is because of number 2. So what does all this mean? Managers have three unique roles they must learn to handle successfully.

Employee Engagement

I realize some people might have labeled employee engagement as the new "corporate buzzword du jour." But regardless of what you call it, the concept of employee engagement is meaningful.

The best definition I've seen for employee engagement is from the global consulting firm BlessingWhite: "Employee engagement lies at the intersection of maximum contribution for the business and maximum satisfaction for employees. It's a sustainable level of high performance that benefits both the company and the employee."[5]

We need employee engagement because it brings maximum contribution to the business. And that's what onboarding is all about—making employees productive so they can bring maximum contribution to the business.

By now, we all realize managers play a significant role in employee engagement and retention. So why wouldn't we make sure our managers are engaged?

Onboarding Has Its Fair Share of Challenges

In the beginning of this chapter, I pointed out Wendy Smith's job title at NCR—leader of new-employee experiences. Some people might scoff that the title is too *trendy*, but one thing it does emphasize is the importance that organizations are giving to onboarding. And justifiably so.

Onboarding is not always easy to do, especially in small firms where having dedicated resources to the onboarding process could be a challenge.

Holger Mueller, principal analyst and vice president at Constellation Research, pointed out the challenge.[6] "Companies give candidates a great recruiting experience; then they have to wait five days to get computer and network access." Obviously, this delays an employee's ability to become productive.

According to the SHRM Foundation's Effective Practice Series on *Onboarding New Employees: Maximizing Success*,[7] research and conventional wisdom both suggest that employees have about 90 days to prove themselves in a new job. That means the faster employees become productive, the faster they can be engaged and successful.

Onboarding Shouldn't Be a Linear Function

In the past, we've viewed onboarding as a linear function of recruiting at one end and engagement at the other (see Figure 2.1).

Maybe we need to view onboarding as a cycle (see Figure 2.2).

Figure 2.1. Onboarding as a Linear Function

Figure 2.2. Onboarding as a Cycle

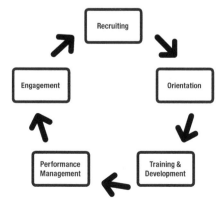

If we do our jobs right with onboarding, we create engaged employees. Engaged employees are productive and maximum contributors for our organizations. They're the people we want to stay and promote into positions of greater responsibility. They are our next managers.

Which leads us to our next chapter and the reason for manager onboarding.

Chapter 3.

Where the Need for Manager Onboarding Might Surface

We've defined the role of manager and the process of onboarding. Before getting into a full-blown justification for why manager onboarding needs to exist, let's identify business situations that create challenges for managers and organizations. They could be called "pain points."

As HR professionals, our first step is to wear the consulting hat. Unless your senior management team has already said, "Create a manager onboarding program," then we have to approach this project with a consultant mindset. I don't mean you should just hire a consultant, although you could certainly do that. Instead, we need to adopt a consulting approach to fixing the problem. In his book *Flawless Consulting*,[1] Peter Block talked about the three goals for consultants:

1. Establish collaborative relationships with senior management.
2. Pay attention to the business problem.
3. Solve problems so they stay solved.

Even though we ~~know suspect~~ believe that manager onboarding will fix the problem, we need to take the time to focus on the business problem before proposing solutions. Years ago, at an American Society for Training and Development (now Association for Talent Development) conference, I heard a presentation by Sears Optical.[2] The company was facing challenges in its retail optical locations. Sales were down, and customer service complaints were up. The first reaction was to implement customer service training. But before doing so, the company spent the time to research the cause of the problem and discovered it needed to do some work with the staff members regarding their roles and responsibilities.

The reason I bring up this story is because I believe manager onboarding is a great thing that organizations need to implement. That's why I wrote this book. But manager onboarding is the answer for *some* things. Not everything. Implementing manager onboarding for the wrong reasons will create the wrong outcomes. Understanding where the pain points are can help the organization determine if manager onboarding is the answer.

How to Determine If Training Is the Right Solution

For training to be successful, it needs to tie back to an organizational goal. Training programs often receive negative feedback not because they were bad programs, but because they didn't fix the problem they were created for. Here's an example: The vice president of operations comes into your office and says, "We need time management training for our supervisors. They just can't seem to get anything done."

Can you offer a time management training program? Absolutely. You could create one yourself, find an online program, or call a consulting company to design one for you. It could be a fabulous program. The supervisors tell you they loved it in the evaluations.

The real question is, did it fix the problem? The answer? We don't know.

Time management could very well be an issue. But how does it manifest itself in the organization? Is it evident that supervisors can't deliver projects on time? Have customer complaints increased as a result? That's the reason training must tie to a business measurement.

After identifying the business metric, it's time to determine if training is necessary. Here are three questions you can ask to determine if training is the answer.

1. Does the person have the skills to do the task?
2. Does the person have the desire to do the task?
3. Is the person allowed to do the task?

If the response to all three questions is "yes," then training is not the answer. It could be an equipment problem. Maybe the reason supervisors aren't able to deliver on time isn't that they have poor time management skills but rather that the copier has been broken for the past two weeks.

If the answer to number 1 is "no," training may or may not be the answer. The answer could be coaching.

A "no" in number 2 means you may have a motivation problem. The supervisors might not deliver on time because the regional manager has told them it doesn't matter how good the project deliverable is, the vice president isn't going to approve it. The supervisors aren't motivated to finish a project that won't be approved anyway.

A "no" in number 3 might mean that there is a policy or procedural issue. What if the reason that the supervisors can't complete the project is that the regional manager changed the scope of the project three times in the last week? The supervisors have no clue what they need to be working on.

So again, while the company might need time management training, it's important to ask a few questions and confirm specific issues before jumping into the commitment for training.

OK. Back to the consulting approach.

Step 1: Establish Collaborative Relationships with Senior Management

This needs to start long before trying to pitch senior management with a program—manager onboarding or otherwise. It is not—let me repeat—it's not a quest for the "seat at the table." Establishing a collaborative relationship means being able to work with others to accomplish the organization's goals.

Building relationships with senior management isn't hard. But it does involve two things. First, it involves speaking in the other person's language. In the case of senior management, that probably translates to using business acumen. I learned this the hard way early in my career.

One of my first manager roles was a one-person HR department for a hotel company. Every week, my general manager held a staff meeting, and his direct reports would go around the table and discuss the projects they were working on and what resources they needed in order to complete the project. The controller would talk about his projects and ask for resources. And he got them. The director of sales and marketing would talk about his projects and ask for resources. And he got them.

The vice president of operations would talk about her projects and ask for resources. And she got them. Then it would come to me.

I would talk about my projects and the resources I needed. Sometimes I got what I asked for, and many times I didn't.

Frankly, it was frustrating! So I spent a lot of time trying to figure out why my colleagues got the resources they asked for and I didn't. One day it came to me. When they talked about their projects, they spoke in terms of dollars and return on investment. When I talked about projects, I talked about what made the employees feel good.

That's not to say that what makes employees feel good lacks value. But I found that when I turned what made employees feel good into a business metric, I received the resources I was looking for too!

HR Metrics and Measurement Resources

If you're looking for assistance when it comes to HR metrics, here are two resources that can help:
- The spreadsheets and calculators section of the Society for Human Resource Management website.[3]
- The book *How to Measure Human Resource Management* by Jac Fitz-enz and Barbara Davison.[4] It's a must-have for your HR bookshelf.

Once we are able to communicate in the other person's language, the second thing necessary to build relationships with members of senior management is truly being interested in them. Human resources can sometimes act isolated because of the confidential information we are privy to and our goal of not appearing as if we're playing favorites.

But being fair doesn't mean that we have to cut ourselves off from the rest of the organization. We ask operational managers to be fair and still get to know their employees. We should be able to do the same.

Years ago, I was chatting with a vice president of human resources who said that she never went out with employees. Under no circumstances. She didn't want to cross that line. I get it. But then I think about those times when I worked in hotels and it was common for managers to get together for drinks after work. They would invite me, so I'd stop by. It never failed that one manager would take me aside during the gathering and say, "I'm glad you're here. I was going to stop by your office. I have this issue." I was able to set up a time to meet with the manager.

If I hadn't stopped by to socialize, I might have never heard about the issue. Granted, maybe the manager would have come by, but when? In time for me to do something about it or when it was too late?

You don't have to hang out and have drinks with everyone all the time. But if you want managers to open up to you, it's essential to show a genuine interest in them. Figure out how to do that.

Step 2: Pay Attention to the Business Problem

If we have good working relationships with others, they will come to us with their problems. None of us likes to admit we are having a challenge. That's why human resources must build relationships with managers. HR cannot be perceived as being judgmental. It needs to be perceived as a solutions provider. It goes back to the consulting approach: Consultants aren't there to judge. They are there are fix problems.

In Step 1, we build relationships with managers. In Step 2, we put ourselves in the position of being a solutions provider. I'm sure you will recognize some of these reasons, but here are the more common situations in which a manager might look for guidance from HR:

Employees that aren't a good fit. You've heard the stories too. Employees who aren't performing to standard, or they just don't fit with the organization. The manager wants to make a change. Now granted, some of those situations are completely legitimate, but in some cases, the solution isn't to terminate the employee. It's to coach the employee. HR can help the manager plan the proper course of action.

Building, borrowing, or buying talent. As recruiting becomes more challenging, organizations will have to ask themselves whether they want to develop talent internally (build), engage consultants or freelancers (borrow), or hire talent from the outside (buy).[5] This is a strategic decision, and managers will be looking to HR to help them understand the talent landscape.

Transitioning from friend to manager. One of the things that companies like to do is show employees they promote from within. It sends the message that hard work is recognized and rewarded. For the employee, though, moving from friend and co-worker to manager can be a big challenge. It's not only a challenge for the new manager but also for the employees—both those employees that the manager is now supervising and the manager's new peer group.

Knowledge management and delegation. As Baby Boomer managers plan their exit strategies into retirement, organizations need to put plans in place to transfer existing knowledge and create a smooth transition for everyone involved. HR needs to play a role in developing a global strategy that will meet the needs of the organization. Finally, managers need to delegate effectively and empower employees so they can learn.

Mergers and acquisitions. Organizations will continue to merge, acquire other entities, and split divisions. Those business activities will create manager positions and possibly even eliminate manager positions. Human resources will be involved in those decisions, redesign the organizational structure, and redefine goals, policies, and procedures.

Unexpected departures (or death). I know this topic is depressing, but it's a reality we have to deal with. A manager that the company thought would never leave comes in one day and resigns. Or announces his or her retirement. A manager has a heart attack over the weekend. Or a fatal accident. The company must figure out how the business will operate without that individual.

Again, these are just a few of the most common situations. The goal wasn't to create an exhaustive list of situations but instead to get us thinking about those times when we want managers to bring human resources into the decision-making process. Managers will bring us into the loop if they feel comfortable coming to HR and confident HR will help them solve their problems.

On a side note, keep these situations in mind as we start to talk about the justification for manager onboarding. Many, if not all, of these situations could be addressed in a manager onboarding program.

The second part of paying attention to the business problem is not waiting for managers to come to us. If we've built a good relationship with managers, we are positioned to inquire about situations that we might perceive as being a problem. Managers might view HR as prying or not trusting if the relationship doesn't exist. When the collaborative relationship is there, however, HR can proactively ask questions or ask for clarification. That might lead to a conversation about the issues we've previously identified.

Step 3: Solve Problems So They Stay Solved

The manager relationships are solid. The challenges are clearly identified. HR is getting involved in the issues where it can have an impact. This is the step in which we use our HR knowledge to solve the problem, not to put a bandage on it.

At this step in the process, we're not doing an assessment. We need to convince the organization that an assessment is the next logical step. Whereas most of the time, we want employees to come to us with both the problem and the solution, at times it makes sense to let a thorough assessment tell us the answer. If you've ever had senior managers come into your office and tell you both the problem and their proposed solution, you know how difficult it can be to talk them out of their proposed solution and into yours. Not impossible, just a lot of hard work—energy that could be spent doing a proper assessment.

On the other hand, I do understand it's hard not to talk about options. Let's use the time management example I mentioned earlier. The vice president comes to your office and says, "I have a problem. Managers aren't meeting deadlines. I think we need time management training." Your response can be, "You might be right, but without a proper assessment, we won't know."

Now, let's add a layer of complexity to this situation. The vice president says, "Yeah, but we don't need an assessment. That will take too long and cost too much." You can now use those three questions I mentioned above. In the role of consultant, you get to share all the options along with the pros and cons for each. You have the ability to earn the vice president's support for an assessment.

At this point, that's the goal—conduct an assessment. The assessment, even a brief one, can save the company money along with producing greater results. Keep in mind that an assessment can also expose vulnerabilities about the manager, the department, and the organization. So managers could be initially hesitant. But when HR is acting as an internal consultant, managers will know that they have a shared goal—to solve problems and keep them solved.

Once HR has been given the green light to proceed with an assessment, it will be necessary to do some homework on the subject. In this case, we need to make sure we understand manager onboarding. The next chapter takes a deep dive into why onboarding is valuable for employees, managers, and the business.

Part II:

The Business Case for Manager Onboarding

"Winning companies win because they have good leaders who nurture the development of other leaders at all levels of the organization."

—*Noel Tichy*

Chapter 4.

The Value of Onboarding in General

In Chapter 2, we defined onboarding. Now let's talk about its value. Obviously, you can see some of its value in the definition, but I think we need to dig deeper. If the goal is to create a manager onboarding program and we want the organization to dedicate resources to it, we need to be able to talk specifics.

For example, the definition of onboarding is "a process that helps employees become productive in the most effective and efficient means possible." Productivity is a value. But what exactly is productivity? It's a state of being able to produce something. In this case, a work output. The value of onboarding is getting employees to produce a work output:

As quickly as possible.

By themselves.

With no errors.

On time.

And within budget.

Onboarding Value on Individual Productivity

The quicker employees know their jobs, the faster they can contribute. We all want to feel we are contributing. It reminds me of McGregor's Theory Y.[1] Employees derive satisfaction from their work, and they want to do a good job. The goal is to make employees productive, so they are happy at work.

Another aspect of individual productivity to consider is the other members of the team. We've been talking about the employee being on-boarded. Chances are, team members are doing extra assignments and working extra hours because the new employee isn't 100 percent productive yet. They will be equally as thrilled when the new employee can carry his or her share of the workload.

In addition to other team members working extra hours and taking on more work, there's a stress factor. The American Psychological Association estimated the cost of job stress to be around $300 billion per year.[2] I'm sure not all of that is attributed to filling in for employee vacancies or temporary assignments, but even if those things account for a small percentage, it's a lot of money.

To help put that into perspective, the Bureau of Labor Statistics said there are approximately 122 million people employed full time in the United States. For the purposes of simple math, let's round that up to say 150 million to include part-time employees and freelancers. That's $2,000 worth of job stress per worker. Think about the implications that job stress is having on the business and the options the organization could employ to reduce workplace stress.

Some of you might be saying, yes—but this information is about new-hire onboarding in general. We're talking about *manager* onboarding. Exactly! If this is the value for new hires and the workplace as a whole, why wouldn't it be the value for new managers? A new manager wants to contribute. And there's a boss, co-workers, and staff who are waiting for the new manager to be 100 percent productive. The work still has to get done.

Onboarding Value to the Workforce

We'd like to think that productivity on its own is value enough. But the reality is, sometimes it's not. Productivity is just the start. Manager on-boarding provides value because it improves employee engagement and retention—not only in terms of engaging and retaining the individual manager but also regarding the employees they work with.

According to the 2015 Deloitte *Global Human Capital Trends* study, companies rated the survey option "retention, engagement, and culture" highest on the list of challenges they faced.[3] Eighty-seven percent of those surveyed rated it as "important," and 50 percent rated it as "urgent." Since this is a book on manager onboarding, it's worth noting that the number two challenge is building a global leadership pipeline.

Recruiting and retaining talent have always been tops on the list of things that keep the C-suite up at night. The issue isn't going away. If organizations want to recruit and retain the best employees, they need competent and effective managers. The way that starts is with proper onboarding of the manager.

We're going to explore this topic more in the next chapter, but let me quickly say that manager onboarding and management development are two different things. Just because a person has attended the company's management development program doesn't mean the manager knows everything he or she needs to become productive. Nor is manager onboarding a substitute for management development. They are both equally valuable.

So the key to engaging workers is to have engaged managers. As such, organizations need to make the appropriate investment in their managers. Surprisingly, many organizations are not making investments in either.

Onboarding Has a Direct Impact on Employee Retention

According to the *2012 Allied Workforce Mobility Survey*, companies lose 25 percent of all new employees within a year.[4] Shocking! Can you imagine what those numbers are today?

In addition, the survey indicated that the average cost to fill one position was nearly $11,000. I have to think companies are more than a little frustrated if they spend $11K to hire an employee only to have that employee leave in less than a year. What's more shocking is the reason why—bad onboarding:

- Almost 30 percent of companies reported that it takes a year or longer for a new employee to reach full productivity.
- Twenty-five percent of companies said their onboarding program did not include any kind of training.
- And 60 percent of companies indicated they don't set any milestones or goals for new hires.

New hires are excited to join the organization. They want to show the company that they are the right candidates. Not providing new hires with the tools and information to be successful, well . . . that makes the new hires wonder why they're there.

The other aspect of the survey that's worth noting was the amount of money dedicated to onboarding. Or more accurately, the lack of it. Approximately 35 percent of companies spend $0 on onboarding. That's not a typo. They spend nothing, nada, nil. I understand budgets can be tight, but to spend $11K on hiring someone and $0 on making that person productive . . . sounds like stepping over dollars to pick up quarters.

While the data from the Allied survey discussed in the textbox above is a few years old, I wanted to share it because it says something about organizational goals and resources. Since the Great Recession, I've spoken to several CEOs who are concerned about meeting organizational goals—not because they don't have the opportunities but because they don't have the talent.

At some point, senior management will be looking for a way to fix this situation. And they will be looking to human resources for the answer.

Onboarding Value toward Organizational Goals

The organization realizes three benefits with onboarding. The first is the one we've been talking about—employee productivity, engagement, and retention. Employees don't want to look for a job as much as the company doesn't want turnover.

Onboarding programs allow employees to contribute. Their contributions (whatever they are) have a positive impact on the organization. No employee does work that neutrally or negatively affects the company. The company just wouldn't have the position in the first place.

Contributions don't have to generate revenue. A contribution could be the absence of overtime. Or an improvement in product quality. Or better customer service. The accounts payable clerk makes sure invoices are sent out on time. The security officer ensures the facility is safe and secure. Every job has value when it is being done properly. And the way to make sure the job is being done correctly starts with onboarding.

The second value for the organization is in administration. I remember years ago having an adjunct teaching position at a local university. At some point, the university decided that instead of their adjunct instructors being contractors, we were to become part-time employees. So we all were sent new-hire paperwork—31 pages of new-hire paperwork. I've heard of companies that have close to 100 pages of new-hire paperwork. Yikes!

Ask yourself how many pieces of paper it takes to hire a new employee or manager? And how many does it take to transfer or promote someone into management? Paper is the bane of human resources. And onboarding, especially electronic onboarding, can provide relief.

The Business Case for Paperless Human Resources

According to The Paperless Project,[5] a grassroots coalition of companies focused on the way organizations use paper, the average office worker uses 10,000 sheets of paper every year. It estimated the cost to file a single document at $20. Organizations spend thousands of dollars each year handling, filing, and storing paper documents.

Even more interesting is that every 12 seconds, a document is lost. The average search time for a misfiled document is 18 minutes. And lost documents cost organizations approximately $350 per document. These numbers don't take into account whether the document is legally required to do business.

To offer some perspective on cost and productivity, let's estimate at how much onboarding-related paper is generated by an HR department using the numbers above. For the average organization with 1,000 employees:

Turnover Rate (%)	# of Employees Onboarded	# Pieces of Paper (31 pieces per employee)	Avg. Cost to File 1 Piece of Paper*	Total
10	100	3,100	$20	$62,000
20	200	6,200	$20	$124,000
30	300	9,300	$20	$186,000
40	400	12,400	$20	$248,000

*Note: This doesn't include employee and company time to complete the form, the cost of supporting documentation copies, and the cost to maintain the files.

This example offers some insight into how much paper on-boarding can generate and the impact one form can have on the productivity of a department. Based on this finding, organizations might choose to implement an onboarding technology solution or to reduce some of the required paperwork. The point is that paper-work costs money and time that could be spent on other things. It could be invested in training managers.

The last value onboarding brings to the organization is compliance. There is a compliance effort to all of our jobs. Many new-hire onboarding programs talk about ethics and anti-harassment. Managers have responsibilities, usually additional responsibilities, in those areas. Onboarding ensures that managers have been given the training to handle compliance issues and reduce organizational liability.

All of the values we've discussed:
- Productivity
- Reduced overtime pay
- Reduced work stress
- Employee engagement
- Employee retention
- Manager engagement
- Manager retention
- Improved product or service quality
- Better customer service
- Efficient paperwork administration
- Effective compliance

Effect the bottom line of the organization. That's the value of new-hire onboarding. And that's the value of manager onboarding.

Before we move on to the next chapter and start specifically discussing manager onboarding, I thought it might be valuable to share how one organization is handling its onboarding programs—both employee and manager. This can offer some creative inspiration as you start to think about your manager onboarding program and how the different pieces would fit together, which is sure to be a question that company leaders will ask you along the way.

I had the opportunity to speak with Dominique Jones, chief people officer at Halogen Software, a leading provider of cloud-based talent management solutions that drives higher employee performance. Dominique was kind to share in detail Halogen's onboarding programs and philosophy. The company has spent a lot of time defining what each component of onboarding means for the individual and the organization. Dominique explained, "Our goal is to lay the foundation for a great, long-term working relationship when welcoming new employees to Halogen. We're constantly enhancing our strategy because our industry changes at a fast pace and to accommodate new dynamics in today's workforce."

Halogen splits its process into two parts—corporate orientation and onboarding.

Corporate orientation introduces new employees to Halogen as a company and is led by part of the HR team. It lasts two days and introduces new employees to the company's culture, strategy, vision, and top priorities for the coming year. New employees also receive a welcome from the executive team members who provide an overview of their core responsibilities and the responsibilities of their team. When possible, the president and CEO delivers a welcome presentation. The goal is for new employees to feel connected to all levels of the organization from the first day.

Halogen also ensures that all new employees receive appropriate training before accessing Halogen's systems or protected information. This includes training about the company's code of conduct and behavior, workplace harassment, legal policies, information security policies, and guidelines regarding Halogen's responsibilities as a publicly traded company. Dominique noted that it's important for Halogen to keep pace with the fast rate of change, so it continually realigns its onboarding materials and keeps existing employees up-to-date by running annual compliance training to ensure all staff is aware of important changes.

Next, Halogen schedules presentations by subject matter experts from across the business to provide a high-level overview of the industry, customers, products, and services. Over the course of the two days, new employees are tasked to set meetings with department members so they have an understanding what each team is responsible for.

Halogen uses a variety of methods to help support new employees. On the first day, each employee is assigned a "buddy." The buddy is a Halogen employee responsible for making new employees feel welcome and for answering any questions. A buddy is not a substitute for the manager, but someone who can answer questions about processes, procedures, and Halogen life in general. There's a social element as well. Halogen sets up a scavenger hunt, and the new employee and buddy are joined by other team members for lunch or after work for social events.

Employee onboarding introduces new employees to their roles at Halogen. There is no set length of time for how long the onboarding period lasts—it tends to depend on the role, the person's experience, and the formal program for onboarding of that particular department. The focus is on enabling managers and new employees to focus on developing into the new role and on providing feedback on early performance on an ongoing basis. In some cases, formal review dates are set at 30, 60, and 90 days. All feedback is documented in Halogen's talent management system. Performance is managed on an ongoing basis, and coaching and feedback are captured in real time.

Sample Onboarding Program for Customer Support

Dominique shared with me an example of how onboarding is carried out by one of the departments at Halogen. This is a terrific example of how onboarding is implemented in an organization and one you can use as you are discussing your organizational onboarding strategy.

Our customer support team constantly receives the highest customer satisfaction ranking from industry analysts. Part of the reason is because employees are set up for success early on in their role and continue to have performance and development opportunities available to enhance their skills. Here's an example of our customer support team's onboarding process for new employees.

On the first day, new employees receive an onboarding development plan through the Halogen Learning™ module within our Halogen TalentSpace™ suite. Onboarding lasts five weeks before support analysts have their first opportunity to speak with customers. During this time period, the customer support team covers processes and procedures, and provides in-depth product knowledge training and an overview of our quality guidelines to ensure new employees understand how to deliver a world-class customer experience. The support team uses tools such as knowledge checks and mock calls to help gauge the confidence level of new employees. If additional training and support is needed, new employees and their managers will invest more one-on-one time to ensure new employees are set up for success.

The support team has a dedicated employee who trains new employees using a variety of teaching methods such as e-learning (computer and web-based training), interactive video, [and] classroom setting, as well as scheduling opportunities to job shadow other more experienced analysts.

The support team is able to measure the success of its onboarding program through key performance indicators such as customer surveys, quality audits, and first ticket resolution percentage (how quickly a new employee can provide a solution to a customer on the first ticket they submit). Once an employee passes the six-month probationary period, the support team manager and trainer provide refresher training and knowledge checks to assess product knowledge retention and help fill any gaps.

Finally, the support team sends out a survey once new employees have been in their role for six months and requests feedback on their onboarding experience to determine what the onboarding program should start doing, stop doing, and continue doing to help improve the experience for future new hires.

Now that you have some sense of how Halogen conducts employee orientation and onboarding, here's how the manager onboarding piece fits in. Dominique said it was important for manager onboarding to align with the company's goals:

"Our corporate orientation and onboarding for leaders is about how we actually live out our mission, vision, and values, and providing them with the tools and resources to relay that to employees."

All managers participate in a training session titled "Manager 101: How to Navigate Halogen's Processes, Structure and Culture." The expectation is that managers understand how to develop talent, inspire and motivate their teams, and lead by example. Understanding what it takes to be a manager at Halogen helps reiterate how much value the company places on the fact that everyone deserves to work for a great manager.

Managers also learn the "business side" of Halogen. They meet with the finance team, which provides training on how to understand company financials. Developing an understanding of how the business functions internally enables managers to set goals and performance expectations for themselves and their teams accordingly, which is a goal management best practice. By keeping in mind how they allocate budget and resources, managers can help employees remain focused on achieving outcomes tied to the goals of the business.

Halogen also believes managers need to understand emotional intelligence (EQ) and different communication techniques at the outset so they are able to customize their approach based on the individual needs of their employees. Part of Halogen's onboarding for new managers is to help them develop an understanding of aspects of the business that are vital for them to know as leaders.

For example, new managers arrange a meeting with their dedicated learning and development manager to help them understand how to set development plans for employees. Learning how to properly create development plans is pertinent because it's directly tied to managing employee performance and being able to establish learning goals, identify appropriate learning activities, and ensure knowledge transfer—all of which contribute to employees being able to advance their careers with the required skills, resulting in a more engaged and high-performing workforce.

Lastly, a critical aspect of Halogen's manager onboarding program is education on how to use the company's approach to employee performance management. Dominique explained the reason:

> We want to create an environment where we are practicing what we preach to our customers and how we go about achieving success and great business outcomes. To this end, each new manager participates in a hands-on walkthrough of our solutions so they can familiarize themselves with our performance management practices within our product. They are then able to transfer this knowledge to their employees, setting themselves up to create a culture of ongoing coaching, feedback, and communication.

If it sounds to you that this is an incredibly robust onboarding program, that's because it is. Dominique said the current corporate orientation program took approximately six months of research and planning. This admission isn't intended to scare anyone. As you're having internal discussions about onboarding programs, it offers perspective.

In fact, one last thing I asked Dominique was whether her team was surprised by anything during the design or implementation process, and she shared that their biggest surprise was also the most satisfying:

The biggest surprise—and most pleasant—was the immediate acceptance of our new corporate orientation program. It can be a challenge fitting new processes into an already busy schedule. The corporate HR team worked together to find the right approach for our new corporate orientation model and it took about a month before all of the details were ironed out. Our administration staff was then ready to hit the ground running with the new program. The feedback about our new corporate orientation program so far has been very positive from all participants, including new employees, assigned buddies, executives, managers, and department leaders.

The Halogen Software example shows us not only the value in onboarding but how manager onboarding has to be treated differently. It's different from orientation, employee onboarding, and management development. In the next chapter, we'll take the conversation to a high level and discuss the situations that justify developing a manager onboarding program.

Chapter 5.

Why Manager Onboarding

In the last chapter, I mentioned that manager onboarding is different from management development. Let's take some time to talk about why they're different. I can see this being a topic of conversation when the idea of developing a manager onboarding program is suggested: "Why do we need that? We have a management training program?" You'll want to be prepared with the answer.

Let's use employee logic in this conversation. No one says, "Why do we have employee onboarding? We have an employee training program." I'd like to think there's a common consensus that general onboarding is important. Whether it's an hour or a day is probably negotiable, but the idea of onboarding is considered valuable.

According to research by Kronos Incorporated,[1] one of the biggest sources of disagreement between employees and supervisors is the amount of time it takes to become fully functional. The data suggest that employees tend to think they are fully productive in weeks versus their managers who say months. Years ago I designed an onboarding program in which we asked this question during the assessment phase and received the same responses with one addition—senior management said close to a year.

This answer is unfortunate because so many organizations wait to provide training to new managers until after an emotional event such as a department layoff, corporate reorganization, manager illness, or death. Without intending to, the new manager is set up to fail. Rita Craig, SHRM-SCP, president and founder of Top Tier Leadership, said, in an interview with the author, smart companies provide the tools for success up front.

When new managers don't get the training they need, it's often difficult for them to get on the right path and gain respect, which is critical to a new leader's success. New managers face the challenge of going from peer to boss in the same organization because one day you're one of them [peers] and the next, you're one of them—leadership!

So, what do smart companies do? They recognize that new managers need training upfront to enable them to maximize their effectiveness. Your duties and accountabilities change overnight and therefore, you may need to adjust expectations, relationships and clarify expectations. The road to becoming a leader is typically paved with lots of challenges. It's important to give yourself some slack and to also have a wise mentor who can help you learn the ropes. Fundamental to success is treating everyone with dignity and respect, modeling the way, demonstrating exemplary communication skills, and learning to delegate!

We talked in the last chapter about the value of employee onboarding—productivity, engagement, retention, so on. All of those reasons are applicable here. Senior management wants to know—why *manager* onboarding? You can present three reasons as being unique to manager onboarding:

1. It aligns with replacement and succession planning efforts.
2. It complements management and leadership development programs.
3. It encourages employees at every level to be more self-managing.

This chapter will focus on how manager onboarding works within your existing programs. Manager onboarding doesn't duplicate existing programs, but it will make your other programs even stronger.

Manager Onboarding Aligns with Replacement and Succession Planning Efforts

According to Pew Research,[2] roughly 10,000 Baby Boomers are entering retirement age every day. Organizations need to be prepared for this change in the workplace landscape. Historical knowledge about the organization, processes, and procedures will be leaving the business, and that loss must be accounted for in some way. In Chapter 1, I mentioned that the goal of every manager is to find his or her replacement. As HR professionals, we need to have a formal system in place to assist managers with this process.

The first step in developing a method of knowledge transfer is to have people to transfer the knowledge to. That means putting some sort of talent strategy in place to replace workers as they make plans to retire. In some cases, businesses will be able to hire the talent they're looking for from outside the organization. And depending on the position, they might welcome bringing in a fresh set of eyes to the company.

But certain roles will have to be developed from within, for a couple of reasons. First, the organization cannot seem to find qualified candidates for those roles, and second, the amount of internal knowledge needed to assume the role is significant, making promotions or transfers viable. Replacement planning and succession planning are perfect tools for the task.

Replacement Planning and Succession Planning Defined

Replacement planning is identifying what the organization would do if it lost a key employee unexpectedly. It could be due to voluntary or forced resignation, death, or disability. Who would immediately step into the role? Ideally, the company wants to identify someone who will need little training to assume responsibilities.

Succession planning is a planned process of identifying individuals who can fill future roles in the organization. The individuals might need training or skills development to fill those roles, and the company works with them to provide development opportunities. The process can take a long time, and the plan is regularly updated to accommodate the company and employee needs.

Having a manager onboarding program tells employees that the organization is invested in their success. I know that statement may seem obvious, but many organizations do not tell employees they're part of the succession plan. So they don't see or understand what the company is doing.

Years ago, I went to work for a company that hired me on the promise that, if I accomplished certain goals, I would be able to move up the corporate ladder. I accomplished the goals, but soon after, the company was acquired, I got a new boss, and those promises were gone. On the day I resigned, my boss said to me, "I'm so sorry you're leaving us. I had such plans for you."

My reply? "Why didn't you tell me? Maybe I never would have left."

One of the most debated subjects in human resources is whether to tell employees they're a part of a succession plan. There are certainly pros and cons to consider. It should be no secret that I happen to be in the "yes, you should tell employees they're a part of the succession plan" camp. My reasons for thinking employees should be told they're a part of the succession plan include:

- Employees need to buy into being a part of the plan. What if they don't want to be a part of the plan? It could happen. It doesn't make good business sense to develop a career plan that the employee doesn't want to pursue.
- Employees need to be accountable for their future. Just because an employee is part of the plan now doesn't mean he or she will remain in the plan. Employees need to be accountable for achieving their career goals if they want to stay in the succession plan.

Being a part of the company's succession plan isn't an employee entitlement. It's an honor that employees earn with work and dedication. And trust me, once you know you're a part of the plan, you have to work hard every single day to make sure you stay a part of the plan.

On the downside, telling employees they're part of the succession plan means you've made the plan public, and it becomes subject to whispers and lunchroom conversation. As a result, several scenarios can happen:

- Some employees will not want to be part of the succession plan. Companies have to be prepared for this response. It may be nothing personal; it's just not a part of the employee's long-range goals.
- Employees who want to be a part of the succession plan and were not identified could become resentful and disengaged. Keeping these employees engaged will be important.

- The company must be prepared to handle situations in which an employee's performance dips and the employee should no longer be considered a part of the succession plan. Awkward? Yes, but absolutely necessary.

I understand the apprehension in telling employees they're part of the succession plan and then the disappointment of telling them they're not. But weigh that against not telling the employees and having them resign for a position with another company with more opportunity.

Succession planning is just that . . . planning. And plans change regularly. For the same reason you should tell employees they're a part of the succession plan, a company should review and update its plan on a regular basis.

If employees don't know the plan, they will be forced to fill in the blanks on their own. Whether or not your organization decides to tell employees they're a part of the replacement or succession plan, manager onboarding sends the message that the company believes the managers are valuable and that it will do what it takes to make them successful.

Another development tool you can consider is talent pools, especially if you're still reluctant to tell employees they're part of the plan. This might be the best of both worlds. Employees know they're being groomed for future opportunities, but the specifics haven't been identified yet.

Talent Pools Defined

Talent pools are groups of high-performing, high-potential employees who are being developed to assume greater responsibilities within the organization. Talent pools are a good approach when you're looking to develop multiple skills or numerous people. An organization might have several different types of talent pools based on its future staffing needs. Examples include emerging leaders, management, and technical specialists.

High-performing (HP) employees are individuals who not only are engaged, but they embrace the corporate culture and perform their current roles at an exemplary level.

> High-potential (HiPo) employees have demonstrated they have competencies the organization values, the ability to obtain the organizational knowledge, and interest to advance within the company.

Talent pools are a great way to think of talent planning when the organization might be reluctant to name a single individual as a successor. The organization develops a talent pool of several individuals. Also, for organizations that are unsure about what future opportunities might look like, but want high-performing and high-potential employees ready, talent pools can be a desirable option. Employees know they have a future with the organization, even if they're not completely sure what those opportunities will look like.

But employees will want to know that, at some point, the opportunity becomes clearer. That's where manager onboarding steps in. At the point an opportunity presents itself, the employee will be looking for assurance that the company will help him or her become productive and successful as quickly as possible.

Manager Onboarding Complements Management and Leadership Development Programs

Don't have a replacement or succession plan in place? You're not alone. In Halogen Software's *State of Succession Planning* report, only 10 percent of respondents said they've prepared current job descriptions "very well" so the work ahead is clear.[3] This finding presents even more of a reason to have manager onboarding as the precursor to your replacement and succession planning efforts.

It's also a compelling reason to have some sort of management and leadership development program in place. As the effects of the skills gap become more prominent, companies will need to take a skills inventory to understand not only the skills they have with their existing workforce but the ones they need to obtain for the future. And then figure out the best way to bring those skills into the organization. Sometimes hiring will be the answer—if you can find and secure the talent.

It's true that both management development and manager on-boarding have a training component to them. But they serve different purposes. Management development programs traditionally give employees the skills to become a manager in the future, the idea being that the employees develop managerial skills prior to receiving the job. And the skills they develop are skills that they can often use prior to becoming a manager.

On the other hand, manager onboarding is about the skills new managers need *now that they have the job*. Realistically, there are topics that make no sense to train managers on until they have the job.

It's doubtful that companies will be able to hire all the talent they're looking for. If they find a great employee, maybe the timing is wrong to hire the person. Or they can't find exactly the right skill set. Or the candidate's salary requirements aren't in the budget. Or a lot of other reasons. Be prepared to implement "Plan B—developing talent" if the talent you're looking for can't be found—or afforded.

When it comes to looking for talent, it might make good financial sense to compare the cost of developing talent internally versus hiring from the outside.

When a company hires an employee, it invests a lot of time, energy, and resources in sourcing, advertising, interviews, offers, and more. Then the new hire goes through orientation and onboarding and might participate in other kinds of company training such as ethics and anti-harassment. The new hire's supervisor spends time talking with the employee about performance expectations, departmental policies, and more.

Cost-Per-Hire

According to research from Bersin by Deloitte, the average cost-per-hire (CPH) in 2014 rose 7 percent to $4,000 per employee.[4] You can calculate your company's cost-per-hire using the formula below. In 2012, the Society for Human Resource Management worked with the American National Standards Institute to develop a universally accepted calculation for CPH:

CPH = (EC + IC) / THP[5]

> Where EC = external costs for all sources of spending outside the organization, including third-party agencies, advertising, job fairs, travel, drug testing, background checks, and signing bonuses.
>
> IC = internal costs such as recruiting staff salary and benefits, time cost for the hiring manager, infrastructure fixed cost, government compliance, and referral bonuses.
>
> THP = total number of hires for the time period being evaluated

My guess is that the number you come up with would buy a lot of training, and probably improve the skill set of more than one employee. Onboarding reduces turnover. Manager onboarding reduces both employee turnover and *manager* turnover. The funds you save hiring new employees can be used in your training efforts.

Manager Onboarding Encourages Employees at Every Level to Be More Self-Managing

Many organizations know only how to operate in an environment of "approvals" or "directives." For example:

- When two employees have a disagreement, where do they go? Either to their supervisor or to HR to solve it.
- If there is a problem with a process, what do employees do? Ask their manager how to fix it.

In a *Harvard Business Review* article titled "Who Is the New CEO?" author Vineet Nayar said future successful CEOs will focus on building decentralized organizations and enabled employees.[6] Businesses are not trying to intentionally build extra layers of management and hierarchical structure. That can be prohibitively expensive. What they want are employees who understand the organization and feel comfortable identifying problems and taking action without a lot of supervision.

The challenge is, how do you do it? Let's face it, the empowerment phase of the 1990s never really caught on long term. The only way to enable your workforce is to teach employees how to become self-managing. Give people the resources to manage their own behavior and hold themselves accountable.

But I'd add—instead of just a high-level theoretical overview of the concepts of self-management, offer employees hands-on tools they can use every day.[7] Include specific sessions on:

- *Problem-solving:* provide employees with a model to solve their own problems.
- *Conflict management:* give employees a method to work out inter-personal conflict.
- *Professional development:* offer guidelines for employees to create their own learning opportunities.

Also, don't assume your management team knows how to supervise a self-managing workforce. This is probably a new concept for them too. Remember to give managers the training they need to successfully manage their employees.

Manager onboarding creates the transition from being a self-managing employee to supporting a self-managing team. Managers need to spend more time on those things that directly generate revenue—and less time on playing referee to their staff. Add to that the impact of gig economics and managers spending their time directing contractors, freelancers, and virtual teams. It only makes sense to give employees the tools to manage themselves—it helps not only them; it helps the company.

It's Not a Replacement; It's an Addition

Manager onboarding doesn't replace the topics being covered in your management development program. Long before an employee becomes a manager, he or she will complete training sessions, and additional training should take place at the time an employee becomes a manager. Manager onboarding allows training to happen at the right moment, so the effective transfer of knowledge takes place.

Manager onboarding will not replace your succession planning efforts.[8] It might help retain employees because they are onboarded well. It might reduce hiring costs because more managers are retained. Manager onboarding makes succession planning successful. It helps ensure that the time, effort, and resources being put into a succession plan aren't lost along the way.

Manager onboarding does help managers do their jobs better and faster. It sets expectations from the beginning about their performance. Managers know what they are supposed to do and can focus on making it happen.

That's what every company wants—to make things happen.

Speaking of which, it's time to make manager onboarding happen in your organization. In the next chapter, we discuss how to sell the program to senior management.

Chapter 6.

Selling the Idea to Senior Management

It might be tempting to assume that convincing the CEO and other senior management is going to be tough, so why bother? This chapter isn't about what to say when selling the idea to senior management. We've already talked about the reasons manager onboarding is valuable to organizations. It's about *how* to sell the idea.

Getting Leadership Buy-In:
An Interview with John Kotter

Change efforts, like creating a manager onboarding program, are futile if they're not supported within the organization. Years ago, I had the privilege of interviewing Dr. John Kotter, Konosuke Matsushita Professor of Leadership, Emeritus at Harvard Business School, about creating organizational change. The secret? Getting buy-in. Here's the interview so you can "hear" directly from Kotter.[1]

Dr. Kotter, from an organizational perspective,
why is getting buy-in so important?

[Kotter] Buy-in is critical to making any large organizational change effort happen. Unless you win support for your ideas, from people at all levels of your organization, big ideas never seem to take hold or have the impact you want. Our research has shown that 70 percent of all organizational change efforts fail, and one reason for this is executives simply don't get enough buy-in, from enough people, for their initiatives and ideas.

Are there ever circumstances when a person shouldn't seek buy-in?

[Kotter] In some situations, you face someone I call a "NoNo." This term is based on a character in my book, *Our Iceberg Is Melting*,[2] which is a fable about life in a changing and turbulent world, set in a penguin colony. NoNo is one of the main characters, and you can imagine how he reacts to any new idea. He not only shoots them down, but is very effective at convincing others to join his side. If you face a group of NoNos—or even just one—seeking their buy-in just won't work. They will continually disrupt conversations and delay action, doing everything they can to discredit an idea and derail processes that attempt to create real change.

NoNos are more than skeptics. If there aren't too many of them, skeptics can be helpful: they can keep naive impulses in check and, once they have been convinced their opinions are wrong, can become an idea's biggest champions. But NoNos won't be convinced. The only way to effectively deal with them is to distract them so they cannot create too many problems, push them out of the organization, or expose their behavior so natural social forces (i.e., other people who want change to happen) will reduce or stop it. My book *A Sense of Urgency* has more information on dealing with NoNos.[3]

What do you say to the person who is reluctant to use buy-in because they don't want to hear criticism or negativity?

[Kotter] I tell them that avoiding attackers doesn't work, nor does quashing their attempts to block support from others. It's far better to respectfully engage these adversaries and stand your ground with simple, convincing responses. By "inviting in the lions" to critique your idea, and preparing yourself for what they'll throw at you, you'll capture busy people's attention, and that's important. Conflict engages. If people have no opinions, no objections, and no emotions, it usually means they don't care. And you'll be hard-pressed getting their help when you have to actually implement your idea. But conflict shakes people up and gets them to pay attention in a novel way. This gives you the opportunity to say why your idea really is valuable and explain it in a way that wins over hearts and minds—securing their commitment to implementing the solution.

The next time you're in a meeting where someone is advocating for an idea, see if some conflict emerges. If it does, watch the group and see how people sit up and the energy level rises. Disagreement may seem like a bad thing—but it grabs people's attention.

What's the biggest mistake people make when trying to get buy-in?

[Kotter] There are a few of them. First, they don't prepare enough. People often misunderstand "preparation" to mean just knowing their own idea forwards and backwards. But rehashing what you already know won't help you avoid sounding defensive, frustrated, or even disrespectful when fielding question after question on your proposal or idea—all things that can derail a conversation and hurt your cause. We often don't even know we come off this way until someone tells us.

> People really need to practice before they attempt to win buy-in from a large group. This means grabbing a colleague to role play, attack the proposal, and practice real-life responses. Try testing your ability to defend your proposal live with select people who will be sympathetic, but who can really listen and provide honest feedback.

I think another key mistake is thinking that you can win people over with lots of data, logic, and reasons why the attacks on your idea are wrong. Almost all education teaches us to think in this manner, but this approach can kill the crucial attention span I mentioned in my last answer. We've all seen eyes glaze over or people surreptitiously typing on their smartphones as meetings drag on and on. You really need to respond to dissenters with simple, clear, common-sense answers—this will slowly but steadily win an audience's minds and their buy-in. And you have to complement this approach by responding in a respectful manner to those who disagree with you, no matter how much you want to fire back with fighting words. Enthusiastic support from large numbers of people is rarely the product of a nasty fight. If you treat the ones who attack your idea with respect, you'll draw more people emotionally to your side. And emotions—what we often call "the heart"—are essential to changing behavior.

From your experience, what surprises people the most
about using buy-in to create organizational change?

[Kotter] I think people are surprised at how well it works. A lot of people who reach senior leadership ranks have been schooled in traditional management training. They recognize a need to change, pick a task force of people (maybe the head of HR, a couple of midlevel managers, a senior VP) to oversee the change effort, assign the team their roles, and instruct them to make it happen. They don't always articulate an opportunity for their organization and then communicate it widely to obtain a broad-based sense of urgency, from employees, to pursue an exciting opportunity, before pressing ahead. When they do, they're often shocked to see how quickly changes can start happening. In our client work, we've found that choice motivates people to be far more committed to driving change than being told they have to do it. It engages people who are passionate about making their organization better, harnesses their enthusiasm, and empowers them to drive change. It's something that seems simple, but it's rare for organizations and senior leaders to work this way.

Six Steps for Creating Organizational Buy-In

Kotter's observations ring true when it comes to creating organizational change, which is why I wanted to share the interview with you. Let me add a couple of observations of my own when it comes to attaining buy-in from senior management:

- I've never met a CEO who was unwilling to listen to an idea that would improve the bottom line. When we talk about initiating change, does the idea improve the bottom line? And if so, how?
- When we talk about creating change and needing support to make change happen, we have to pitch those ideas in terms that everyone understands. Bottom-line results? Everyone understands bottom-line results.

Remember the story I mentioned earlier about attending the weekly manager meeting and learning how to talk about HR projects in terms of numbers? When I was able to talk about what the employees wanted in numerical form, I was able to get the project and resources approved. That's why I waited until Chapter 6 to talk about selling the manager onboarding idea. Now, don't get me wrong. Senior management does care about employees' feelings and their engagement with the organization. But before selling this idea, HR professionals need to accomplish the following:

1. Learn how to calculate internal metrics.
2. Understand the key metrics for your organization.
3. Keep current with external business trends.
4. Anticipate potential objections.
5. Find a project sponsor.
6. Estimate the budget.

Let's cover each in more detail.

Learn How to Calculate Internal Metrics

I've already mentioned it once, but one of the must-haves on my business bookshelf is *How to Measure Human Resource Management.*[4] Don't know how to calculate something? This book will show you. The important thing to remember is that your internal metrics remain consistent. No one asks the chief financial officer (CFO) if he or she always uses the same formula for calculating profit.

Understand the Key Metrics for Your Organization

Every industry has them. They are the metrics that set your organization apart from the competition. Speaking of competition, it might also be necessary to understand regional metrics in addition to industry metrics, especially if talent leaves your organization for another employer in your city but not necessarily in your industry.

Keep Current with External Business Trends

Indicators such as unemployment rates, and demographics factor into everyday business decisions. Find reliable sources of business data, and read them regularly. The source you use could be dependent on your industry or local geography, such as the local economic development board, or related to your profession, such as Leading Indicators of

National Employment (LINE) from the Society for Human Resource Management.[5]

---

3 Resources for Labor Data

Finding data can be easy. The challenge is finding *good* data. Here are a few resources to bookmark:
- Bureau of Labor Statistics (BLS): www.bls.gov
- Pew Research Center: www.pewresearch.org
- U.S. Census Bureau: www.census.gov

These sites have lots of data, and they also have links to similar sites. Let's say you need state labor market information. The BLS has a list of non-BLS sites to help you find what you're looking for.

Convincing the CEO and senior management to embrace a change or new program doesn't have to be hard. It does take staying on top of business trends, which we should be doing anyway. And it takes communicating the change in a way that everyone understands, the language of bottom-line results.

Anticipate Potential Objections

When planning the conversation with senior management, think about any potential objections that might come up and how you would respond. This point reminds me of a conversation that I had with Mark Simpson, vice president of Legendary People at Texas Roadhouse.[6] If you're not familiar with it, Texas Roadhouse (aka Roadhouse) is a full-service, casual dining restaurant chain. The company operates over 400 restaurants in 48 states and three countries. Its motto of "legendary food, legendary service" has led the company to be recognized as one of the Employee's Choice Best Places to Work by Glassdoor and one of America's 100 Most Trustworthy Companies by *Forbes* magazine.

I met Mark at a workshop where he shared with attendees how Roadhouse changed the company's annual performance review process. As HR professionals, we know how contentious the annual review has become.

Mark said the senior leadership team had been trying to figure out for some time how to separate the performance appraisal process from merit increases. "When performance and pay are tied together, it creates an emotional conversation. We wanted to change the performance discussion to become more productive and constructive."

Interestingly, Mark said he found the answer in an unsolicited e-mail with a subject line about killing the performance appraisal. The e-mail shared details from the book, *Get Rid of the Performance Review!* by Samuel A. Culbert.[7] After reading the book, Mark decided to share it with the office to see what others thought.

In case you were wondering, Texas Roadhouse is an organization with a bottom-up structure. The corporate offices aren't called that—they're called the support center because they "support" operations. When a decision is made, the question is asked, "What do our operators think, and how will it affect them?" because according to Mark, "they are the center of our universe. They are the reason we're profitable and successful."

After yielding a positive reaction to the idea of changing performance appraisals, a management team was formed to build and implement the new system. Managers were chosen because they understood both sides of the performance appraisal process. They gave reviews, and they got reviewed. Mark said it was this team that sold the new process to the president. "It became a project driven by our people, not an HR initiative."

Mark's story reminds me that every change initiative doesn't have to start with human resources pitching an idea to senior management. Potential objections can be worked out by discussing the idea with managers. In fact, that could be a fabulous idea—let your managers who would have wanted a program like this when they were hired or promoted help sell the program for you.

Find a Project Sponsor

In formal project management, the project sponsor is the senior management person responsible for making sure the project remains active and garners the resources it needs. Project sponsors don't typically work hands-on with the project. Their expertise is used in a different way, providing influence and positional power to keep the project on track.

7 Types of Workplace Power

Everyone has power and using power isn't a bad thing. The issue is what kind of power a person has and how someone uses that power.

Webster's New World College Dictionary defines power as "the ability to control others; authority; sway; influence." So in essence when we use power, we're using our authority to get something. Here are the seven types of power found in the workplace:[8]

- *Coercive* power is associated with people who are in a position to punish others. People fear the consequences of not doing what has been asked of them. Anyone, not just one's immediate boss, can wield coercive power by assigning an unwanted task or unfavorable schedule.
- *Connection* power is based on who you know. This person knows and has the ear of other powerful people within the organization. Connection power is associated with networking and relationship building.
- *Expert* power comes from a person's knowledge and expertise. This is commonly a person with an acclaimed skill or accomplishment, not necessarily one with Ph.D.-type smarts. It could be the person who has the magic touch fixing the copier.
- A person who has access to valuable or important information possesses *informational* power. This person could be at any level in the organization.
- *Legitimate* power comes from the position a person holds. This is related to a person's title and job responsibilities. You might also hear this referred to as positional power.
- People who are well liked and respected can have *referent* power.
- *Reward* power is based on a person's ability to bestow rewards. Those rewards might come in the form of job assignments, schedules, pay, or benefits. The boss is not the only person who has reward power.

Now, don't be modest and think to yourself . . . I don't have any power. As you can see, power can manifest itself in many different ways. And for that reason, it's important to realize that power exists in everyone. It's also possible that you have different kinds of power with different groups or situations.

The two biggest mistakes people make using power revolve around (a) trying to use power they don't have and (b) using the wrong kind of power to achieve results.

To help you identify your "power zone," take a moment and think about how you try to influence action from others. You could use the descriptions above as a pseudo self-assessment. Rate yourself on a scale of 1 to 5 in each of the different kinds of power, with 1 being not at all characteristic of you and 5 being quite characteristic.

This can be a (sorry for the pun) powerful exercise. If you're honest with yourself, I hope you will find the results helpful—not only for the way that you tend to use power but in the way others use power with you.

That being said, with a project like manager onboarding, it's important to remember this is a company program. It could make some sense to have project co-sponsors based on the influence needed to champion the program. The idea of co-sponsors also adds another benefit—if one sponsor becomes busy or sidetracked, the other sponsor can continue to help champion the effort.

The project team should be composed of those roles that will do the work and turn the idea of manager onboarding into a program. Ultimately the new program will affect every department. However, that doesn't mean that everyone needs to be on the project team. Consider the roles (versus people) that would be ideal for the project team. It's possible that senior management will want to know a few details about how the program will be designed and implemented. By responding with roles rather than with specific people, it demonstrates to senior management that the plan has been thought out, but it doesn't raise objections about individuals and their skills and workload. That can be dealt with later once the project is approved.

Estimate the Budget

Being able to build a budget is a valuable skill. It shows the organization that you can be a true business partner, and you will learn a lot about the company by participating in the budgeting process. As I think back on my HR career, I learned about budgeting in pieces—a little bit here, another piece there, so I thought it might be valuable to offer a high-level overview of how to build a budget.

I can see projects like a manager onboarding program being something that is pitched and considered during the budget process. While the conversation about developing a manager onboarding program might start well before the annual budget process, at some point someone might say, "This is a great idea, but we don't have the money in the budget." Your reply should be that the plan is to include the program in the next budget cycle, knowing that the next budget cycle isn't too far away. Following are the eight steps to assembling a project budget.

Step 1: Know the budget calendar. Every organization I've worked for had a budget calendar. It outlined when budgets were due, when budget reviews took place, and when department managers would learn their budgets were approved. Having a clear understanding of the process is important. During your annual budgeting process could be the perfect time to ask for funds for a new manager onboarding program.

If your organization doesn't have a formal budget calendar, find time to talk with your chief finance officer. Ask him or her to share with you the specifics of how the process works. You want to know when to start the manager onboarding conversation so it can be included in the budget.

Step 2: Review prior budgets. Before starting a new budget, take a moment to review what happened in the past. Understand what was budgeted for in prior years and how accurate those budget amounts were.

- Did you budget a lot of funds for something that wasn't spent? Why wasn't the money used?

- Did you not budget enough funds for something? Why did you exceed budget?

In the case of manager onboarding, it might prompt the need for extra research about other training and management activities, but it's worth it. If you have to justify your budget numbers, then you will want to know this information. Trust me.

Step 3: Establish goals. With previous years in mind, now it's time to finalize goals—both for the department and the program. We want to make sure that we have the financial resources to accomplish our goals and objectives. Also keep in mind the feedback you've received from other departments and what they will expect as a result of the program being approved. And don't forget to meet with the HR team members about their individual goals that will affect the department budget.

Step 4: Identify capital expenditures. Most of the time, as an HR professional, I had few capital expenditures. But it's possible that you might have more (depending on the design of your program). Capital expenditures are incurred when the business spends money on fixed assets. An example would be property, plant, or equipment. If you have a question about whether a budget request is a capital expenditure, ask the members of the accounting department. They will be happy to tell you.

The capital budget is like a budget within a budget process. The capital budget is separate from the operating budget, but goes through the same reviews and approvals as the operational budget.

Step 5: Create the budget. Now that you're ready to start putting numbers into the budget, it's time to understand how your organization creates budgets. There are two types of budget strategies:
- Incremental budgets are based on adjusting the current budget. For example, "We spent X dollars per employee on orientation last year, so budget that we will spend 5 percent more this year."
- Zero-based budgeting means that every item on the budget must be justified. Past budgets are not considered in the process.

While manager onboarding is a new program, it's possible that the organization might use existing orientation and onboarding expenses as a guide. As you think about your budget line items, remember a few key areas:

- Revenue: An increasing number of HR departments are generating revenue. They sell training programs to third parties or allow tours of their organization (for a nominal fee). HR isn't always an "expense only" department anymore. Is it possible to generate revenue with this initiative?
- Expenses: Unlike some departments, HR has two types of expenses: (a) costs that affect only the HR department and (b) costs that affect the entire organization. You'll want to consider each carefully and work with finance to make sure your budget submission reflects both.
- Staffing analysis: I've worked for a couple of companies that charged back recruiting expenses to each individual department, but for the most part, recruiting is an HR expense. Having a current staffing analysis will help develop and justify your recruiting budget. Will program costs be charged back to each department?

Step 6: Know where you have flexibility. Some people will call this step "sandbagging." It's when you add money to your budget knowing it will be cut in the review process—so you end up where you wanted to be all along. Although I cannot officially condone sandbagging, I can unofficially tell you the process exists.

I'm not bringing this up to encourage manipulating the budget. I am mentioning it because, at some point, you will be asked to tweak your budget numbers, especially with a new program like manager onboarding. Be prepared and know where you can make adjustments without sacrificing quality.

Step 7: Look for budget support. Once your budget is finalized, you will want to have supporters. These could be the project sponsors, if they eventually review and ultimately approve the budget. They may not be able to give HR everything it wants, but make sure your supporters know what the top one or two goals for the program are so those funds don't get cut.

The art of creating a budget is essential to human resource management. We're the experts on HR, so we should be responsible and accountable for how much it costs. Budgeting isn't always the most fun activity, but it's one in which you will learn a lot about the organization and build valuable relationships with the rest of the business. Oh, and there's one more thing . . .

Step 8: Monitor your budget regularly. After the budget is approved, create a process for reviewing expenses to ensure you stay on track. If your organization has a regular P&L (profit and loss) review meeting, ask to be invited to it. You will learn a lot about financials and the company.[9] And, don't be surprised if, at some point, you're asked to reforecast your budget. That's taking this process and rebudgeting (only in a much smaller timeframe).

Building the Business Case

When I think of presenting a business case, a tried and true outline is using the scientific method. I know many of us haven't thought about the scientific method since our school days, but it does provide a logical way of outlining a business problem and possible solution.[10] As a reminder, here are the steps to the method:

1. *Identify the problem.* The first step in the scientific method is to identify and analyze a problem. The scientific method works best when you have a problem that can be measured or quantified in some way. Data regarding the problem can be collected using a variety of methods, which we've talked about (for example, HR metrics, workforce demographics). It's about sharing the answers to the classic questions: who, what, where, when, how, and to what extent?

2. *Form a hypothesis.* A hypothesis is a statement that provides an educated prediction or proposed solution. A good format for a hypothesis would be, "If we do X, then Y will happen." Remember, the hypothesis should be measurable so it can help you solve the business problem identified in Step 1.

3. *Test the hypothesis by conducting an experiment.* This is when an activity is created to confirm (or not confirm) the hypothesis. Entire books have been written about conducting experiments. We won't go into that kind of depth, but keep in mind that your experiment could be a pilot group or a phased-in rollout of a new program.

4. *Analyze the data.* Once the experiment is complete, you can analyze the results. The results should confirm the hypothesis as either true or false. If by chance the results aren't confirmed, this doesn't mean the experiment was a failure. In fact, it might give you additional insight to form a new hypothesis. It reminds me of the famous Thomas Edison quote, "I have not failed. I've just found 10,000 ways that won't work."

5. *Communicate the results.* Whatever the result, you should communicate the outcomes of the experiment to the organization. This will help stakeholders understand which challenges have been resolved and which need further investigation. It will create buy-in for future experiments. Stakeholders might also be in a position to help develop a more focused hypothesis.

Now let's use the scientific method for our manager onboarding example.

Step 1 (identification): Human resources has noticed an increase in resignations over the past six months. Exit interviews indicate that employees do not feel their managers support them and their work.

Step 2 (hypothesis): If we provide a manager onboarding program, fewer employees will resign.

Step 3 (test): For the next six months, HR will provide all managers in the operations department who are hired, transferred, and promoted a half day of manager onboarding. Topics will include communication skills, productivity tips, and leadership training.

Step 4 (analysis): After six months, HR has seen a decrease in employee resignations in the operations department. But there are still comments about lack of manager support.

Step 5 (communication): After communicating the results, the company is examining the following options:

a. Expanding the program to include other departments.
b. Expanding the program content to include other topics.
c. Using blended learning to deliver onboarding content over a longer span of time.

I've found using the scientific method to be helpful in situations like the one we're talking about here. A person or small group has a theory about how to solve a problem, but it's possible that not everyone has accepted the theory. Offering the option to test the proposed solution, without a full commitment, tells the group members that their suggestion is being heard and that the numbers will ultimately provide insight—after the full scientific method has been followed.

Selling the idea of manager onboarding is the process of logically and methodically securing buy-in. Do the research and gather the data, think of the potential objections, find project sponsors to champion the program, build a budget, and finally present the business case. Each step builds on each other. Every step shows that the program is valuable and can yield results. So don't be surprised when the program is approved. You've worked hard to get senior management and the rest of the organization onboard. (Pun intended.)

Now, it's time to deliver.

Part III:

5 Steps to Developing a Manager Onboarding Program

"The secret of getting ahead is getting started."

—*Mark Twain*

Chapter 7.

Assessment

Conducting an assessment is an essential step in the process of creating a manager onboarding program. The information you've collected to date—all the metrics and demographic data—was not the assessment.

Back in Chapter 3, I mentioned developing a consulting approach, and in step three, solving problems so they stay solved, we talked about assessments—specifically, when the assessment should be completed.[1] That moment is now.

It can be tempting once the program receives the green light to just forge ahead without conducting an assessment. Senior management might say, "You've convinced us. Go ahead and create it." And that's terrific. Or someone might say, "We know the program will be great for our managers. Assessment isn't necessary." And it's true—the program will be great for managers.

It will be even *better* once you complete the assessment.

The purpose of the assessment is to take a structured look at the manager skills that the organization needs along with the skills that the managers currently have. The key word here is *structured*. There's a good chance you have a working knowledge of the skills that the organization wants to develop in the manager onboarding program. It's also possible that you and members of the senior management team have a good sense of the skills your current management team possesses. But do you have all the information?

I learned my lesson about assessments the hard way. When I first became a consultant, I was hired to conduct a day of training to managers about communication skills. I asked the organization about doing an assessment, and the response I received was, "We know what we need, and this is it." So I said okay and developed a day of communication skills training.

On the day of the training, the managers were engaged and excited to be there. But they wanted to talk about employee coaching, which granted, is a form of communication—just not the communication that my contact in human resources had described. Luckily, we were able to have a conversation about both. But the training clearly would have been better if a proper assessment had been completed.

Assessments don't have to be long or expensive. Remember the consulting approach. The goal is to do enough without doing too much. Just between us, plenty of organizations give consulting a bad name with their assessment process. This causes people to cringe at the mere mention of the word assessment. Assure your senior management team that the assessment will be comprehensive without getting out of hand. Then manage the length and depth of the assessment. A couple of things to remember:

- If you're planning to use a pilot group or a phased implementation, you will have the opportunity to make certain changes in the program. Obviously, you don't want to make big changes to things like content topics or delivery methods, but you do have the ability to change things.
- Evaluations will be regularly conducted. This is another opportunity to make adjustments in the program. Over time, it's possible that whole sections of the program will be changed and updated. So it's important to remember that the program will be dynamic in nature.

I once worked on a project team to create initial technical training for new-hire employees. We were under a serious time crunch to produce the programs—I'm talking only weeks to produce over a dozen training programs. I remember having a conversation with our project team leader about assessments. We still did them, but when it came time to actually develop the training, we kept in mind that the programs were going to be modified over time. That's what happens in a dynamic workforce.

Instructional System Design Models

While this book will not be providing a deep dive into the nuances of instructional systems design (ISD), I do want to use a familiar ISD model for developing this program. The ADDIE model is a generic framework for designing training. It was developed years ago by Florida State University for the U.S. Army. Because the model has been around for years and is known for its proven ability to be repeated easily, I'll use that model in this book. The ADDIE model has five phases (see Figure 7.1):

1. Analysis
2. Design
3. Development
4. Implementation
5. Evaluation

Figure 7.1. ADDIE Model

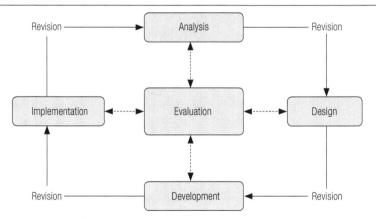

> **Successive Approximations Model**
>
> If you're not a fan of the ADDIE model, another ISD model gaining in popularity is the successive approximation model (SAM). The model uses agile development methodology, which is the idea that evaluations are done regularly throughout the design process.[2] This keeps the design from going off track both in terms of budget and time line.

Over the next five chapters, we'll talk about each of the five phases in the ADDIE model. The ADDIE model can be used conceptually for any type of program development. So if the organization decides to develop a manager mentoring component for its manager onboarding program, you can use the ADDIE model to develop the program. Just think of it in terms of the mentoring piece.

However, my guess is that most manager onboarding programs will have some sort of formal training session contained within the overall program. This would be similar to the orientation session contained in a new-employee onboarding program. So we will talk about ADDIE in terms of developing that formal training program. Just remember it can be used for any other components in the onboarding program.

In this chapter, we'll focus on assessment. To keep the process simple, assessment has two parts:

1. Conducting a needs analysis, so we know what the organization will need in the future.
2. Conducting a skills inventory, so we know what managers are currently capable of doing.

The goal is to bring these two pieces together to find those topics that the existing system currently addresses as well as those areas that are not being addressed and need to be added. There's also a third outcome that could surface, and that's the notion that the company is conducting training it no longer needs. Hopefully that's not the case, but it is within the realm of possibility. (If by chance the company discovers it's conducting training it doesn't need to do, then stop. Save the organizational resources. You'll need them later for something else.)

Conducting a Needs Analysis

The organization might already have some documents in place that will help with a needs analysis. The company's strategic plan offers insight into future critical needs. The annual operations plan might address short-term challenges that need to be addressed. If the organization does a SWOT analysis as part of its planning, the weaknesses and threats sections could be of assistance.

SWOT Analysis and Appreciative Inquiry

A SWOT analysis is an activity that allows the organization to identify its strengths, weaknesses, opportunities, and threats (SWOT) from a business perspective. It's often used during strategic planning and represented in a grid format. Strengths and weaknesses are focused on the internal organization. Opportunities and threats are focused on the external organization.

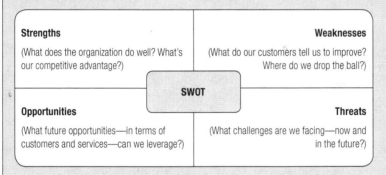

A downside of the SWOT analysis format is that some cultures might spend too much time focused on the negatives (that is, weaknesses and threats) and not enough time on the positives (that is, strengths and opportunities). An alternative is the process of appreciative inquiry. Simply put, it's the process of imagining what the future should look like and developing a plan to get there.[3] Both processes are widely used and can be valuable in offering organizations a candid look at their strengths and opportunities.

The purpose of reviewing existing documents is to figure out what the organization has already committed to in terms of future needs. For example, if the organization has a plan to grow by acquisition over the next couple of years, that would be important to know. Or if the company plans to discontinue one product line and add a new line, that would also be helpful to know. Reviewing existing documents offers some insight about the needs of the organization.

After reviewing what documents currently exist, one of the most straightforward ways to conduct a needs analysis is by administering a survey. One of the easiest and most effective assessments I've done was a short telephone survey with participants for a management development program. Not only did the participants appreciate having the opportunity to weigh in, but we were able to incorporate some of their comments into the content. It also gave me (as the eventual facilitator) the opportunity to start building a relationship with the participants. While several data collection methods exist, a survey is advantageous for several reasons:

- *Inexpensive.* Surveys today can be done using no-cost or low-cost online tools.
- *Large number of responses.* Because the survey can be administered online, it's able to accommodate a large number of responses, which is great for creating buy-in.
- *Quantitative and qualitative questions.* Survey tools give you the ability to use several different types of questions: rating scales, yes/no responses, checklists, and open-ended.
- *Quick to administer.* Once the survey is designed, it can be distributed via e-mail.
- *Easy to compile results.* Depending on how you structure the survey, the data can be downloaded into an Excel file for tabulation.

Sure, surveys have several advantages, but they do have drawbacks—the biggest being question development. Ask good questions, and you'll elicit good responses. Ask garbage questions, and well, you know what you're going to get.

> ### *Data Collection Outcomes*
>
> We spend a lot of time talking about quantitative data. That's the objective, measurable, and, most often, numerical data. Quantitative data are great because they can help identify trends and patterns. They also allow for a conversation about issues without identifying specific individuals—the data can be aggregated.
>
> But that doesn't mean qualitative data aren't beneficial. A story can be compelling. The opinion of a subject matter expert can carry significant weight. In thinking about data collection, consider what information is best presented via numbers and what information would be best told anecdotally.

Sample Needs Analysis Questions

When developing the questions for your needs assessment, think on three levels: (1) What is the business need?, (2) What's the department need?, and (3) What are individual employee needs? Here are a few questions to consider:

Business need questions
- What are the company's goals over the next two years?
- What do customers tell you about the company's product or service?

Department need questions
- What are the departmental strategies needed to support the organization?
- How do you measure those strategies?
- How do you know when there's a problem with the strategies?

Individual employee need questions
- What does excellent performance look like?
- What knowledge and skills might prevent employees from performing as they should?

At this point, information has been collected and organized, and you know what the future needs of the company will be over the short-term and, possibly, the long-term. The next question to ask is, what do you currently have in terms of organizational talent?

Conducting a Skills Inventory

Remember in Chapter 2 we defined knowledge, skills, and abilities. The purpose of a skills inventory is to determine skills. Critical to the success of the onboarding program is to make sure you're focused on skills because skills can be learned. If you focus on knowledge, that doesn't necessarily mean that the new manager knows how to do anything; it simply means the manager has the knowledge. And if you focus on abilities, it means the new manager has the qualities to do something, but it's possible the manager isn't using the qualities in that way. Focusing on skills means the manager onboarding program is focused on those skills that can be learned.

Conducting a Task Analysis

For each manager position in the organization, conduct a task analysis. This is a process in which you learn the individual tasks being performed by a job and how they are accomplished. There are several things to determine:
- Why is the task completed (that is, task objective)?
- How important is this task?
- What does it take to complete a task?
- What supporting knowledge or skill is necessary?
- What is the performance standard?
- How does the manager currently learn this task?

I know this sounds like a lot of information to gather. And it is. But you do have some flexibility in the way you collect the data.
- *Survey.* I bring up survey because you've already trained the organization on how to do surveys with the needs analysis. So a survey might be the best way to acquire this additional information.

- *Observation.* It might be possible to observe how managers perform their jobs. A word of caution that this method could be time-consuming.
- *Interviews.* Similar to a survey, a structured interview question-naire could be given to the manager. It allows for additional questions based on the manager's response.
- *Brainstorming.* This is a one-off of the interview scenario. Similar to a focus group, the managers are brought together to develop responses in a time-controlled setting.

After the needs analysis and skills assessment are completed, you will need to compare the two. And the best way to do this might be with a spreadsheet or table. Table 7.1 is an example of what you might come up with.

Table 7.1. Comparison: Needs Analysis and Skills Assessment

Organizational Needs	Manager Skills	Gap
The organization plans to open 3 new locations over the next 5 years. Managers will need to be able to hire, train, engage, and retain employees.	Managers do not receive any type of interview skills training. All departmental training is done on the job. On the last employee survey, employee engagement was at 58%. Current turnover is at 30%.	• Interview skills • Department training • Employee engagement • Employee retention
New technologies are being introduced that will require the organization to make major equipment upgrades to remain competitive.	Current employees do not have the skills to operate this new equipment. Managers will need training on the equipment and on how to train employees.	• Technical training • On-the-job training
90% of the current senior management team is of retirement age. There is no replacement or succession plan in place.	On the last employee survey, scores were low in the areas of promotional opportunities. Over the past 6 months, 3 managers have been hired by the competition.	• Management development

Of course, this example lacks some of the details you might gather from your internal assessment, but you get the idea. At the end of the assessment, you will have a list of topics to potentially focus on when de-signing your manager onboarding program. Notice I used the word "po-tentially." It's possible that, when we reach the next phase—design—the organization will not be able to include everything in the onboarding program. That's reality. It doesn't mean the program will be unsuccessful. It does mean that skills might need to be developed outside of the manager onboarding program, possibly in the organization's management development program.

There's one additional outcome that you should have been able to achieve through the needs analysis and skills assessment—an audience analysis. Hopefully as a result of these two activities, you have a good sense of who the audience will be for your manager onboarding program. The audience analysis will tell you who the typical participant will be in terms of age, gender, education, professional background, cultural background, and other characteristics. If you are unsure about the answer at this point, take a moment to ask more questions. It's difficult to write an effective learning program if you don't understand who you are writing it for.

Before we move on to the next chapter and the design phase of the project, here's a quick recap of the steps to conduct the manager onboarding program assessment.

Step 1: Needs Analysis

- Review any existing documentation regarding the organization's plans.
- Administer a survey to obtain information directly from stakeholders about the needs of the business, departments, and employees.

Step 2: Skills Assessment

- Conduct a task analysis to determine the tasks managers need to know, how they should be completed, and what skills are needed.
- Include stakeholders in gathering the information.

Step 3: Identify the Gap

- Compare and contrast the results of the needs analysis and skills assessment to identify the gap.
- Document outcomes to determine the most appropriate topics to include in the program.

Chapter 8.

Program Design Options

Once you've completed the assessment, it's time to develop goals and objectives. You'll want to develop a goal for the overall manager onboarding program then objectives for the individual components of the program.

Sometimes in traditional instructional design, you might see the development of goals and objectives in the assessment or analysis phase. I like including it with program design because, realistically speaking, the goals and objectives for the program will be considered at the same time as program design. We don't always have an open checkbook for projects, and our goals will reflect that. Also keep in mind that the goals of the program can change over time. So there's nothing wrong with setting a small goal with the idea that, in the future, you can expand the program.

Before we dive into goal setting, let's briefly talk about a topic that usually comes up during the design options phase—adult learning principles. To design programs that new managers will learn from, it's necessary to understand the principles of adult learning. Here are three principles to remember as you develop your program goals and consider design options:

- *Adult learners must be motivated.* The managers in this program already have a lot of knowledge and expertise. So for learning to be successful, it needs to be something that the individual wants to learn. The topics must be relevant and interesting.

- *Adult learners must be self-directed.* Chances are these new managers didn't get where they are because someone told them what to do all the time. They will want a say in their own learning activities. When individuals understand how they learn best, they can decide if they want to learn via a book or a podcast or a conference. They have control and responsibility for the information.
- *Adult learners want problem-centered content versus subject-centered.* Learning must fix a problem or help achieve a goal. Learning cannot take place for the sake of learning. This ties into the other two principles. Individuals must be motivated to fix the problem or achieve the goal. And they need to feel that the learning will help them be successful in their career.

How to Set Goals

As you consider program goals, remember the key to success is creating and managing them properly. Here are four things I keep in mind when I'm setting any kind of goal:

- *Create a realistic number of goals.* I'm a fan of stretch goals, but this is a new program. You want to create a win. It's better to have a small number of goals and achieve them than hundreds of goals that are left undone.
- *Set goals that are relevant.* If you create a goal based on what the cool companies are doing, it's not really your goal. It's their goal in your company. Base your goals on the data you discovered during the analysis.
- *Establish a manageable timeline for achieving your goals.* I'm convinced part of the reason organizations don't accomplish their goals is because they try to start too many projects or initiatives at the same time. Schedule goals over a span of time.
- *Allow for flexibility as conditions change.* As dedicated as we may be toward accomplishing our goals, sometimes external forces decide to wreak havoc. Instead of beating ourselves up because our goals aren't progressing, we should step back and reevaluate the goal. It could be that the goal is fine, but we just need to give it a little bit more effort. Or maybe the goal needs tweaking.

How to Develop a Learning Objective

One of the most essential and challenging components to designing training is creating the learning objective.[1] If you've been a part of designing a training program, you know it's one of the first questions asked—"What's the program objective?" And weak objectives don't sell the value of the program.

Weak objectives use weak verbs. Words like as *know*, *learn*, *understand*, and *appreciate* are examples of weak verbs. Here are a couple of weak learning objectives:

- Understand the four components of a learning objective.
- Be able to describe the four components of a learning objective.
- Our workshop will provide participants with the opportunity to learn the four components of a learning objective.

Now, please don't hate me for saying it. We all know it. And I'll admit, on occasion, I've used those weak verbs myself. *But there's a better way.* I use what is called the A-B-C-D method for developing an objective.

Audience. This is fairly self-explanatory. They are the participants.

Behavior. This is the "thing" they need to know or do.

Condition. This represents the support that is provided to the learner. It might be a book, job aid, etc.

Degree. This refers to the required efficiency level.

Here's an example:

Given a complete copy of the book on setting performance goals, the participant should be able to accurately describe the four steps for setting a performance goal without error when offered at least three opportunities to do so.

In this example:

A (Audience) is "the participant."

B (Behavior) is "accurately describe the four steps for setting a performance goal."

C (Condition) is "given a complete copy of the book on setting performance goals."

D (Degree) is "without error when offered at least three opportunities
to do so."

By just asking these questions, this four-step process is a thorough
way in developing an objective.

1. Who is the intended learner?
2. What does the learner need to know or do?
3. What kind of support will we provide? And lastly,
4. What is the degree of proficiency the learner needs to have?

With your program goals and objectives set, it's time to consider
the different delivery options available. We will talk about classroom,
on-the-job, mobile, social, and microlearning options.

Classroom Delivery Isn't Dead

Yes, it's true. Classroom delivery is not on the decline. Now you might
be thinking, "Hey, why all this talk about mobile and social?" or "How
come e-learning is so popular right now?" And it's true—training departments are discovering new methods. But that doesn't mean the old
methods are dying.

According to Brandon Hall Research, classroom delivery has increased about 5 percent over the past few years based on its "Relationship
Centered Learning" research.[2] The number isn't huge, but it's not a surprise. In my experience, I've found that classroom delivery is starting to
serve more than just a training purpose. It allows companies to create
reward and recognition opportunities. Senior management can spend
time with participants and begin to develop relationships. That's perfect
for a manager onboarding program.

I've also seen HR use classroom delivery as a way to solicit feedback
from participants about projects it's working on. Think of it as a casual
focus group.

When we talk about value in mobile and social, I often hear that
the real value comes when people get the chance to take their online
interactions into real life. And this trend carries over into the classroom:

virtual teams getting the chance to meet each other. Employees from all of the world connecting in person, then collaborating online.

The key to making classroom delivery successful is to understand if there are "additional goals" for the event. These might not be formal learning objectives as much as they are event objectives. For example, the organization will bring in a special presenter over lunch or senior management will have breakfast with the group. Trainers and facilitators need to build time for these interactions to take place. And smart companies are finding ways to use trainers in the activities.

Purist training professionals might not like training sessions being watered down with other organizational activities. Personally, I see it as a wonderful enhancement to the overall experience. It brings senior management into the classroom. It gets participants talking about what they've learned over dinner and drinks—after the session, of course. HR is brainstorming ideas with participants. All good for individuals and the company.

On-the-Job Onboarding

For smaller organizations that might not have new managers on a regular basis or companies with a large virtual workforce, it might be necessary to consider delivering on-the-job training (OJT) for manager onboarding. On-the-job training is one of the oldest forms of delivery, and if designed correctly, it can be effective.[3]

Before we talk about the components of OJT, let's quickly discuss just-in-time training (also known as JIT). The whole concept of just-in-time training is that an employee learns something just in time to use it. That's a valuable and good use of resources. There's no sense in training new managers on how to conduct interviews if they aren't going to use the information for six months. By the time they need it, chances are they will have forgotten it. So there is a just-in-time component to on-the-job training. But all just-in-time training does not have to be conducted on the job. It could be just-in-time classroom training. For example, conducting a webinar on how to deliver performance appraisal feedback at the start of the performance review cycle would be just-in-time training but not on-the-job training.

For on-the-job training to be successful, there are three aspects to consider:

1. *Management support.* OJT does not mean training is free. Organizational resources still need to be allocated toward material development and learning time.

2. *Trainer support.* Not everyone can deliver OJT. The organization needs to identify the right people to deliver training and give them the tools they need to be successful, such as a train-the-trainer program.

3. *Administration.* A system needs to be put in place to keep track of training completion. OJT training is still learning, and, if the company keeps track of other programs, it will want to keep track of this one too.

Onboarding in a Box

LinkedIn's talent solutions division offers a downloadable guide to developing "onboarding in a box." While the guide is for general new-hire onboarding, I can see this being used as creative inspiration for developing a manager onboarding version. It includes information to help employees on their first day, first month, and first quarter.

I particularly liked the "Best Boss Ever" checklist. It's a list of little things that a new hire's manager could review with the new employee over coffee, like how to order office supplies and reserve a conference room—things you usually find out how to do because you do them wrong and someone corrects you.

In addition, the list has an "awesome extras" section loaded with ideas to make employees' first days special, such as bringing them a swag bag with company logo items and giving them a welcome card signed by the team.[4]

Mobile Learning Is about the Participant, Not the Device

When it comes to mobile learning or m-learning, the "m" stands for "me" as the participant, not "mobile" as in the technology. Of course, mobile devices are involved, but that's not the reason to create a learning opportunity. The learning is driven by the needs of the participant.

M-learning is about me learning something specific, in a bite-size chunk, at the moment I need it. Think of it as just enough, just for me, just in time. When you think of m-learning in this context, it might frame the reason an organization would decide to use mobile as part of a manager onboarding program.

The device doesn't drive the discussion. For example, just because everyone has a mobile device is not a reason to create m-learning. What drives the discussion are the content and how participants will use the content. The content must address a gap—which takes us back to our findings from Step 1, our assessment (in Chapter 7.)

Everything is not an m-learning project. Yes, mobile is cool. And apps are cool. But, similar to the process we go through to decide if a program should be in a classroom or e-learning, the same type of conversation needs to happen with m-learning. It could be tempting to create an m-learning project because someone in senior leadership is enamored with the idea of having an app. But ultimately, the project will not be successful if m-learning isn't being used for the right reasons.

User adoption is key. So let's say the company does go through with creating m-learning. Before starting the project, it's essential to gather information about the targeted users for the learning. Find out how they currently use their mobile devices. Also ask them what their favorite apps are and the reason. The last thing any company wants to do is spend time and resources creating an m-learning initiative only to find that people aren't using it.

It's true that m-learning is widely popular because of the widespread adoption of mobile devices. Lots of companies will be exploring m-learning as a result. But we have to put our business hat on and make sure we are allocating resources properly.

Social Recruiting Sets Expectations for Social Training

According to a Jobvite 2014 social recruiting survey,[5] over 90 percent of companies used social recruiting as part of their hiring strategy. Now call me crazy, but it seems only logical that if companies are using social media as part of the hiring process that employees will expect to see it once they get hired.

It makes no sense to hire someone using Twitter, then tell the new hire in company orientation that Twitter is banned. It sends the wrong message on day one of employment. This applies to both managers and employees.

Employees who are hired using social media tools will expect to see social media in training. Companies building a brand presence on social media will want their employees to connect with the brand via social platforms. It enhances employee engagement. The question becomes how to create effective activities that support the learning objective.

Here's an example using photos—smartphones with camera and video capability, camera and video editing apps, and social sites that support sharing images:

> One of the ways we learn is by visuals. We can create powerful learning experiences by using the right images at the right moment. This not only applies to technical training, where we can take photos of actual equipment or shoot a quick video of how to do something, but it also applies to soft skills.

Another example is during your next management training program, you asked participants to take a photo that validates your company culture. They all have those smartphones—right? In fact, instead of begging and pleading with managers to put their devices away . . . send them out on an activity using them. Ask participants to upload their photo to a site and debrief the photo collection as a group.

Social media is firmly engrained in our business culture. As individuals do more with social media in their personal lives, the expectation that social tools will be incorporated into an employee's career will increase. Initially, it might seem easy to introduce social tools into the learning experience.[6]

But like everything that's done during training design, finding the right tool for the best outcome can be a challenge, especially when you consider the pace at which social tools are changing. That doesn't mean to avoid social media in your manager onboarding program. It does mean to choose to research options carefully.

5 Reasons to Consider Microlearning

Microlearning appears to be new to the scene, and I'd say it's worth paying some attention to it. It's defined as small learning units or bite-sized pieces of content. It's different from the other forms of training we've talked about so far because it's intentionally designed to be small, so it's going to work for some pieces of the program but probably not for all the pieces. Here are a few things I've learned about microlearning:

- *It's easy to produce.* Please notice I didn't say cheap. Microlearning is shorter than standard training programs and therefore should be cost-effective to produce, but it may not be an inexpensive option. Still, microlearning topics may be less complex to design and implement than traditional e-learning projects.
- *It's flexible.* Microlearning can be classified as "on demand" if participants can access it whenever and wherever they wish. It could also be called just-in-time training if it's used to refresh/remind/teach employees something immediately before they need it. For example, a manager may want to review the steps of counseling an employee right before meeting with him or her.
- *It fits today's technology.* One of my mantras when designing is to make stuff easy to buy, easy to use, and easy to share—meaning that people who are trying to engage with the organization shouldn't get the runaround. Because microlearning is focused on a single concept, it can be created using a simplistic process, and it can be easy for the company to share and easy for employees to view.
- *It can complement your existing programs.* I've already mentioned microlearning being able to provide a refresher or reminder. It can do that as a follow-up to a traditional classroom learning experience. Instead of searching for a printed participant guide, an employee can search for the microlearning session. It can provide a solution in a moment of need.
- *It could be a coaching tool.* I think of coaching as being able to help employees reach their goals. Part of helping them could be offering them resources that will improve their skills and knowledge. Managers could use microlearning as part of their employee

coaching toolbox. When an employee is stuck and needs some assistance, a manager could recommend microlearning sessions.

As you can see, there are many different ways we can learn. That's a good thing because participants can find a learning method that they connect with. I also understand that justifying the time and resources to create all these different learning methods may be difficult from a corporate learning perspective.

That being said, the new methods emerging right now—concepts like mobile, social, and microlearning—have tremendous flexibility and can bring a return on investment in more ways than one. Something that classroom training might not be able to do. It doesn't necessarily mean we need to ditch classroom training—it means consider adding different methods for variety.

Selecting the Facilitation/Training Team

Another option to weigh—before actually starting to write content—is who will be delivering the program? Or, more specifically, who will be delivering each piece of the program? It's possible that individuals within a program team will be assigned a certain piece of the program based on their knowledge and expertise.

The knowledge and expertise of the trainers will drive the content delivery. You know your workforce, so you can determine who is qualified to handle each topic. But I emphasize the importance of giving trainers the tools to do their jobs, especially if the individuals chosen were selected for their technical expertise. Consider conducting a train-the-trainer program or supporting their participation in an organization like Toastmasters so they can get comfortable with their role and presenting information—whether that's for 5 people or 15 people.

Facilitation Skills for Virtual Instructors

Train-the-trainer programs are great for developing classroom training skills. One area we should talk about separately is virtual training. Just because a person is an awesome classroom facilitator doesn't mean he or she will be an equally awesome virtual classroom instructor.

Let me wander off the beaten path for just a second and point out that virtual classroom facilitation isn't the same as a webinar. The goals for each are different. Virtual classroom instruction is like classroom training . . . but virtual. And even though I'm describing the experience for the participant like it's "classroom training on your computer," that doesn't mean that the facilitation piece is the same as classroom training.

Obviously, content knowledge and participant engagement are essential in both situations. But there are a few additional areas in which we have to shift our focus for virtual instruction:

- *Technology.* Not only do we have to know the technology we're using, but we need the ability to talk and use the tools at the same time. With virtual facilitation, points on the screen may need to be highlighted or placed on the whiteboard while the discussion continues.
- *Nonverbal communication skills.* In the virtual classroom, participants can't see our body language. Speaking clearly and with confidence is key. In addition, we have to be able to change tone, inflection, and pace to communicate effectively.
- *Participant interaction.* Both classroom and virtual training need participants to interact, but we have to remember to allow for silence in virtual classrooms. In the classroom environment, we can see when participants are processing information. We have to allow for the same in a virtual setting.
- *Questions and discussion.* Virtual facilitators have to become comfortable calling on participants by name to contribute. In the classroom environment, a facilitator can pose a question to the group and elicit responses. Participants can raise their hands and take turns. This is difficult to do virtually.

As technology and training become even more commonplace, it might be necessary to develop trainers to be effective in delivering virtual training. We cannot simply take one set of skills and expect them to transfer completely. Adjustments must be made for participants to have a good learning experience and, more importantly, for the training objectives to be met.

Media Selection Options

In this last section of the design process, organizations will want to explore all the different types of media they can use to develop content. One way to think about developing content is in the context of the way people like to learn.

Auditory learners would be interested in lectures, discussions, books on tape, podcasts, and study groups.

Visual learners would enjoy photo imagery, mind maps, flowcharts, and diagrams.

It's possible both auditory and visual learners might like video. You can both see and hear the presentation.

Kinesthetic learners would be interested in role-playing, field trips, writing, games, and activities involving movement.

Learning Styles Myth

In an article from *Nature* titled "The Science Myths That Will Not Die,"[7] there's mention that the notion of learning styles is a myth. Specifically, the article says that the following is a myth: "Individuals learn best when taught in their preferred learning style." The author does point out a couple of truths associated with learning styles:

1. Many people do have a preferred way for how they like to receive information.
2. There is evidence to suggest that the best educational outcomes occur when information is presented in multiple modes (that is, visual, auditory, and kinesthetic).

I'm not here to take on the science community about learning styles. I will say that learning is about communication and information. And I agree with the author that each of us has a preferred way of receiving information. I'd even add that our preferred way might change depending on type of information. For instance, I might

---

prefer reading business subjects and hands-on training for cooking topics. It might also be possible that our preferences change over time—my learning preferences as a college student are different from my preferences today.

The point is that we cannot take a single test or assessment that will determine our preferred learning style and use that style forever in all situations. The importance of learning styles is for designers to create programs using multiple methods and for learners to receive information using multiple mediums. It's even possible that we could learn more by venturing outside our comfort zone and receiving information in a nonpreferred style. As learners we have to be open to that possibility.

What designers, facilitators, and learners have to balance is using the "step outside your comfort zone" option, but not as a way to force an uncomfortable learning experience. Most of us like learning in a safe environment. Learning involves making mistakes. So the reason a learner might embrace the concept of a preferred learning style is because it provides comfort and safety.

As you're thinking about the design of your manager onboarding program, consider varying the methods. In addition, managers need to be capable of self-learning. This doesn't mean simply learning what the company tells them. It means having a high-level understanding of what they need to know, how they need to learn it, and what resources are the best to accomplish the task.

Combining a lecture with the opportunity to practice could appeal to all three learning types. The auditory learner hears the lecture, the visual learner sees the presentation, and the kinesthetic learner gets to practice the activity.

No one activity will accommodate all three, but a well-designed program will offer variety that will give each participant the chance to connect with the content.

When it comes to designing manager onboarding (or any kind of learning program), the great news is you have options. And lots of them! Don't let the process overwhelm you. The assessment you completed in Chapter 7 is your guide. It will lead you toward the right delivery method, the best trainers, and finally, the media you should select.

In the next chapter, we'll dive into actual content development. Before we do, here's your quick recap for understanding your program design options.

Step 1: Conduct an audience analysis.

- Understand the demographics of your management team.
- Visualize how the managers want to learn.

Step 2: Consider the different types of training (classroom, mobile, social, on the job, microlearning).

- Match the type of training to the content.
- Consider budget and development time in the decision.

Step 3: Select the training team members and give them the tools to be successful.

- Consider team teaching.
- Have back-up facilitators.
- Give them training, including facilitation skills training.

Step 4: Explore the various types of media. Be sure to use a variety of activities that will appeal to everyone.

- Create activities that allow participants to see, hear, and do.
- Be open to using technology in the training (that is, smartphones and mobile devices).

Chapter 9.

Development Strategies

During the development phase, you'll actually create the content that will be delivered during manager onboarding. And now you have the necessary details to do that. In Step 1—assessment—you identified the audience and skills gaps. In Step 2—design options—you completed the research to determine the best delivery method along with plans for the training delivery team.

We still have decisions to make, but they will be based on the information we've already gathered and driven by the decisions we've already made. For example, one of the first decisions we have to make in this phase is who is going to develop the content. Basically, you have two options:

- The content can be developed internally. The upside to this approach is that the person working on the content has knowledge of the organization and can customize the training to the organization. The downside is that it's easy for the project to get put on the back burner because that person probably has other responsibilities he or she needs to complete.
- The content can be developed externally. This can be advantageous because an external consultant can work on an accelerated timeline. If it's a consultant who the organization works with regularly, he or she may have the organizational knowledge to customize the deliverable. The downside, of course, is cost. An external consultant could be an extra expense.

Whether you use an internal or external developer, the organization will also want to evaluate how much custom work will be done versus using an existing product and possibly making minor adjustments. For example, will the onboarding program include in-house developed videos or off-the-shelf videos? Depending on the point you're trying to convey, one could be better than another. But they are substantially different from each other in terms of cost and development.

Custom content is generally more expensive to produce, but it's also more connected to the organization's brand. In my experience, it makes sense to use custom videos when talking about aspects of the business that you want to showcase, such as customer service and employee recognition. The content not only makes its point but instills a sense of pride. One thing to consider when developing custom content is how it will be maintained. Let's say a video includes a message from the president, but then the president leaves the organization . . . well, the video needs updating as soon as possible.

Off-the-shelf content is more generic, so it's less expensive and can potentially have a longer shelf life. One potential exception to the cost issue is if you decide to use movie or television clips and need to seek permission. Regardless, it might take more facilitator training skills to introduce the content and connect it with the company's operation. While off-the-shelf content might not instill a sense of organizational pride, it can bring some sense of fun and whimsy to the program.

How to Manage the Project Timeline

I mentioned above the possibility of the development falling behind schedule. Something unexpected happens—like getting an illness that slows you down, having your computer hard drive go kaput, or having other projects come along that need immediate attention. It happens to the best of us. Being behind schedule doesn't mean the project is over. The important part is getting the project back on track.

It was years into my professional life before I took my first project management course. If you haven't taken a course, at least try to pick up a project management book so you can learn how to build and maintain a realistic project timeline:

- Identify all the tasks that need to be completed.
- Budget for all the resources necessary to complete the project.

- Prioritize the work.
- Assume delays will happen.
- Consider your normal project schedules.

Once you've got a rough timeline in place, commit to the timeline formally. What I mean by this is budget time for it on your calendar. A project of this magnitude will never get finished if you work on it only when nothing else is happening. We're all busy, so allocating time is critical.

If you don't already have favorite project management software to help you formally schedule out the project, here are a couple of suggestions:

- Microsoft Project is a software program that offers the ability to produce a project timeline, including resource allocation, instant messaging within groups, and team collaboration. The software has multiple versions to accommodate your project management needs.
- Basecamp is a cloud-based software program that offers users the ability to create checklists with deadlines, upload project documents, and invite multiple users to a project group. It offers apps so you can follow the status of your project on any device.

The key to selecting project management software is to find what works for you. Don't purchase something because it's the hot new trendy program on the market. There's an old quote by celebrity chef Alton Brown, "Organization shall set you free." I know he's talking about being organized in the kitchen, but the same applies here. Your project will stay on track if you're organized. So find the method that works best for you.

At this point, you've put together a reasonable timeline and committed it to your schedule. Now it's time to realize that, at some point, there will be a challenge. I'm not trying to burst your bubble here. Just being realistic. The good news is, if you don't encounter any challenges, think about how pleasantly surprised you will be.

However, if you do have to deal with a delay or multiple delays, establishing a good timeline to start will not derail your project too far. In my experience, if you have an unrealistic timeline to begin with—and then a delay occurs—that's when the project can get off track.

When a project does experience a delay, you are in control of how to fix the situation. Here are a few questions to ask:

- What is the reason for the delay?
- Do you need or want to extend the project timeline?
- Should you hire an outside consultant to assist with the project?

Using effective project management tools allows you to stay focused on the entire project and make good decisions when adjustments are necessary. And trust me, you will have to make adjustments along the way.

Developing a Content Map

Once you're satisfied with the learning objectives, methods, and media being used in the manager onboarding program, it's time to focus on the content. The goal is to create some sort of flow chart that encompasses three levels:

1. The manager onboarding program in its entirety. So let's say a new manager will have a one-on-one meeting with his or her boss, then attend a half-day program, then be assigned a mentor. You'll want to create a content map that shares the flow of the overall program.

2. Within the program, there's a half-day session. You'll need to create a second map for that. The half-day program might include administrative things managers need to know and serious legal considerations, just to name a few.

3. Then within the session, you'll want to break down topics. For example, the legal considerations portion of the workshop might include handling investigations, union avoidance, and other topics.

Mapping is the process of visualizing what your program will look like. Think of it as a roadmap of where the manager will go in the program. When you get down to the session level, the map should also include initial thoughts about the visual elements and text. It can identify where activities will be included. The idea with mapping is to put your concept together visually and *then* start developing it.

Mapping Tools

There are several ways to map out your program. You can create a map on a flip chart or whiteboard. Just make sure no one erases it! I've also seen maps on index cards or sticky notes, which makes it easy to move ideas around. And in today's technology age, you can use apps for mapping. Do an Internet search for "best mind mapping apps," and you will find dozens of articles helping you choose the best app for you that's compatible with your devices.[1]

Clearly, mapping is important. The last thing you want to do is start building a program and go back and forth during development. Mapping allows you to work out the flow and hopefully minimize errors. Once you begin mapping, you will find that you have a process that works for you. However, there are a few best practices that can help the mapping process.

Give mapping the time needed. Even when we have a clear vision in our heads regarding what the final program will look like, we need to map out the content. I often find little details that I need to change or want to add during the mapping process. Mapping allows me to set the design to the side for a few hours to gain new perspective. This isn't a step to rush.

Also, mapping doesn't have to be a solo activity. Consider involving your subject matter experts in the process. You will need their expertise in determining the level of detail needed to cover during the onboarding program. And you will want their buy-in if they are ultimately going to deliver the program.

Polish previously used content. Let's be realistic—we want to create content that we can use again for other projects. In fact, not having to create entirely new content is the beauty of training. That being said, when we do incorporate previously used elements, we need to update them to fit the project we're working on.

Mix it up! While we do want our project to have a certain branded look and feel, the course doesn't have to consist of one font, one color, and one background. Figure out creative ways to use your branding elements to keep users interested in your visuals.

Edit the content. Don't overload a screen with too much text and or too many figures. If the screen appears too busy, the content will be hard to comprehend, and that will affect the success of your program. Consider separating concepts into multiple pages and using click-to-reveal actions to help users actively process information.

Have a defined proofreading and editing process. Once your map is complete, do a self-proofread of your work to pick out any grammar or punctuation changes. Then give it to a colleague to review. Having a fresh set of eyes on your map can be a valuable asset. You're going to want to have a dedicated proofing process for the content; use the mapping procedure to set that up.

A detailed, completed map finishes your planning process. At this point, all the key elements have been discussed and decided. The pages have been tweaked and reviewed. Now it's time to build the course.

5 Steps to Learning Any Topic

When it comes to content, you can use this five-step outline to deliver a topic, whether it's to one person or 100 people.

Step 1. Introduction

Start out by telling participants how this training will benefit them. This is also known as the WIIFM (What's in it for me?). When people have a clear and reasonable understanding of why they're in attendance, they are more likely to participate. Most of the time, when people don't pay attention in training, it's because they don't understand the reason they need to learn the topic or skill.

The next item to accomplish during the introduction is finding out what people already know about the topic. There are three reasons you want to understand this:

Focus on the right information. If all the participants already know a piece of information, you don't have to spend as much time on it. You can quickly cover it, leaving more time for other parts of the training. An example would be if you're conducting a training meeting on the steps to create a mail merge within a word processing program. The participants are all familiar with the proper way to create the database file, so instead of spending a lot of time on it, a brief review will suffice.

Clear up any incorrect information. Sometimes participants have information about the topic, but the information is incorrect. During the review, you can determine if participants have the correct information and address any misinformation.

Solicit the knowledge of others. Often organizations conduct recurrent or refresher training. These are short programs designed to remind people about a subject. Customer service is a great example. A training meeting might be focused on telephone standards to deliver quality customer service. Employees who have been through prior trainings can be a source of information. Instead of training to them, train *with* them.

Step 2. Demonstration/Discussion

This step is the actual transfer of information. This is when the learning happens. You can conduct this step two different ways depending on the purpose of the meeting.

If the meeting is about something that people do, then it's best to conduct a demonstration. One way to know if the topic is something people do is to think of it in terms of "how to." Some sample topics would be:

- How to coach an employee.
- How to deliver a presentation.
- How to properly complete an expense report.

When it's necessary to give a demonstration, be sure you are prepared and have everything you need for the demonstration. This includes following a logical sequence when doing the actual demonstration. There's nothing more frustrating than watching someone conduct a disorganized, ill-prepared demonstration.

Another step to remember is to make sure all the participants can see what you're doing during the demonstration. Being visible while you're explaining and performing the steps can help ensure participants understand them.

The other topic is what people *know*. It could be considered information or facts. The best way to conduct the training meeting is with *discussion*. Example topics include:
- Four ways to recognize employees for a job well done.
- Employment application instructions for callers.
- Proper communication during a workplace emergency.

These are topics that don't necessarily need a demonstration. For instance, you can share with people the process that applicants should follow to apply with the company without anyone physically completing an application. But participants might have questions about the process. There could be a discussion about how to handle various scenarios. The point is to convey the information and encourage discussion about how to use it effectively.

Step 3. Testing/Practice

Whether you conduct a discussion or a demonstration, it's necessary to test participants and ensure they've learned the topic. If you have a discussion, then you can test participants on the information. This can be done formally using a pen-and-paper test or informally with a verbal question-and-answer session. The topic might dictate the best approach. Compliance-related training might require a formal testing procedure. You should know what your organization requires.

If you conduct a demonstration, you can ask participants to physically model the task. When it comes to participant demonstrations, here are three things to keep in mind:

Allow the most inexperienced person to go first. Having the most experienced person go first creates an intimidating training environment. When the least experienced goes first, there's an opportunity to build confidence for everyone.

Don't interfere. It might be tempting to help the person giving the demonstration. Resist the urge! Taking over the demonstration takes away the person's confidence and sends the message that he or she is doing it wrong. Your role is to provide support.

Ask participants to describe what they are doing while they are doing it. Just as you explained the steps while doing the demonstration, ask participants to do the same. It confirms that the participants know the steps even if the demonstration is awkward.

Step 4. Feedback/Debrief

After the testing/practice step, conduct a debrief or feedback session. Debriefs are an opportunity to discuss those things that went well and what can be improved.[2] Research from the Group for Organizational Effectiveness shows that teams that conduct debriefs perform an average of 20 percent better.[3] The debrief itself can be as simple as:

- What did you do well? Or what went well?
- What would you do differently? Or what would you change?

After discussion and testing, you can ask the group what topics were easy to remember and why. Another question would be to find out how people remembered a topic—what strategy they used to recall. On the flip side, you can ask the group what topics were a challenge to remember and what methods the participants might use in the future to keep them top of mind.

By contrast, the feedback process after a demonstration has a bit more structure. Here are the three steps:

1. Always ask the participants for feedback first, asking them to tell you what they did well. As humans, we sometimes focus too much on what went wrong. It's important to celebrate our successes, especially when we're learning something new. Don't rush an answer, even if it means allowing for a little silence.

   When it comes to the participants providing feedback on what they would change, encourage them not to view their actions as "wrong." A training environment should be a safe place to practice. That's why the demonstration was done.

   The reason you allow the participants to provide feedback first is because, as a general rule, the participants will be far more critical of their performance than anyone else. This positions the rest of the group to be supportive rather than critical.

2. Then allow the group to respond. Most groups will not focus on the negative feedback because the participant has already mentioned it. The thought is "they know it; I don't need to bring it up." The group

members will offer supportive comments. Why? Because they want supportive comments when it's *their* turn.

3. And lastly, as the trainer/meeting organizer, you give your feedback last. This is a great opportunity for you to support the participants. You can add any positive feedback the participants didn't cover, offer suggestions for next time, and express your confidence in their ability.

Step 5. Wrap-up or Closing

To wrap up the training meeting, review all the key points of the topic. Make sure participants clearly understand what is expected of them back on the job and tell them what to do if they have any questions after the session.

These five steps can be used in a short 30-minute session or a full-day workshop. Introduce the topic, explain why it's important, share the relevant information, give the participants a chance to practice, offer feedback, and wrap-up.

You and your subject matter experts will determine the topics and the information you want to share. Later in the book, I'll offer a few suggestions that you can consider, but you're the experts on what makes a manager successful in your organization.

This chapter is about creating a structure to develop content for the program. The best way is to view it like a project. Here's a recap:

- Step 1: Bring together the content development team, including subject matter experts and possibly external consultants.
- Step 2: Establish a project timeline and anticipate potential time obstacles.
- Step 3: Use content maps to outline the information that will be in the manager onboarding program and any training sessions, as well as the content within the sessions themselves.
- Step 4: Use the five steps for delivering content to finalize your content.

Now the program is ready to be delivered. Well, almost. A few more finishing touches are necessary. Your manager onboarding program is a high-profile addition to the organization. It would be helpful to work out a few kinks prior to officially launching it. That's what pilot groups are for.

Chapter 10.

Pilot Programs

Before the manager onboarding program is rolled out to the entire organization, it can be beneficial to conduct a pilot program. Pilot programs are like test runs to make sure that everything works and flows smoothly. Even the best-designed programs may need a little tweaking.

Plan to make the pilot special. This first group of participants will wear two hats for you: both as managers attending the program (for its content) and as people who will give you feedback (to improve the program). You will also want to seek feedback from the delivery team as well as the managers' bosses.

This isn't to say that, after the program is implemented, you'll stop soliciting feedback from participants, trainers, and supervisors. But this first round will be a little different.

Selecting Participants

Think carefully about the individuals you want in the pilot program. You want the group to be able to both participate and evaluate at the same time. You also want to know that the group will not hesitate to provide honest feedback.

Depending on the number of managers in your organization, the pilot could be one group from a single department or a variety of people from different departments. Using one department could be helpful with scheduling or getting one senior manager to buy in to the content. However, variety of people could bring more diversity of feedback.

While it might be tempting to keep the naysayers out of the pilot group, consider having at least one individual with the ability to challenge the system. If those employees are excluded, they will make sure that everyone knows they were excluded. And any criticism of the program is an opportunity for them to say, "If I had been there . . ."

I do understand that sometimes those individuals can be a pain. They can also be the people who push the manager onboarding program to a higher level. And the other employees know who these disrupters are. If one of those devil's advocates start talking about how great the program is, that's a valuable endorsement.

Training Logistics

Planning and logistics are important for all training but especially for the pilot group. External factors can have an impact on the program, which will affect the outcome. The person conducting the training should take an active interest in meeting logistics.

As a training professional, I'm reminded of it every time I plan a training session. I often say, "The mind can absorb only what the rear can endure." Think about it. It's true. Logistics is the first key to any meeting's success. Here are some logistics issues to think about when planning a meeting:

- Logistics letter: It's possible that, for manager onboarding, people will need to travel to a central location for activities. When people need to travel for your meeting, consider drafting a single logistics letter providing instructions for traveling from the airport to the hotel or office, a list of restaurants in the area, and other helpful details. Sending a dozen short e-mails with information is not an acceptable substitute. Yes, you've disseminated the information, but it's a pain to organize! Supply participants one page with everything on it—keep it simple, and participants will love you for it.
- Prereading or prework? Tell participants in advance if they are to read or review something beforehand. Sending a book, article, or PowerPoint before the event is not an automatic directive to read something. Be sure to set a clear level of expectation.

- Welcome: Prepare a welcome for the event. Even with groups that work together on a regular basis, the welcome can also serve as a way for the members to reconnect since their last meeting. I like having participants do mini-interviews as an icebreaker. They are amazed at what they didn't know about their colleagues.

- Agenda: Do not assume that participants printed the meeting agenda and brought a copy with them. Make enough copies for everyone.

- Visitors: When you have people who travel in for your event, keep in mind they might not know the city or the building. Employees at the host location should sensitize themselves to their visiting colleagues and answer what might seem to be obvious questions.

- Views: I recently attended a meeting where a large pole blocked my view of the speaker. Shame on me for sitting behind a pole. Shame on the event for putting a chair there in the first place.

- Comfy chairs and working equipment: Uncomfortable chairs make people cranky. Cranky people do not make for good meetings. And if you need equipment during the meeting, make sure it works. Have a backup plan in case it breaks down. Murphy's Law is always an option at *any* meeting.

- Wireless: This is the 21st century. Everyone wants access to Wi-Fi—even in training. If you have visitors attending your meeting, set up a guest account and password. Tell people how to access Wi-Fi prior to the meeting starting. Put the passcode on the agenda. My guess is that bad or a lack of wireless access is the top pick in meeting complaints.

- Refreshments: Despite what anyone might tell you, refreshments are important. I'm totally convinced refreshments tell people how much you care. For short meetings, a few beverages or at least pitchers or bottles of water could be enough. For longer meetings, snacks and possibly meals need to be considered. Even if you decide not to provide refreshments and you personally can live with skipping lunch, keep in mind that not everyone is the same. Participants might even have health issues they need to address by eating regularly scheduled meals.

Meeting Room Set-Up

Speaking of chairs and meeting room logistics, a decision you need to make when conducting training is the room setup. The layout of the room should align with the content of the training. Depending on the topic of your training, some room layouts are better than others. Figure 10.1 provides a few of the most common layouts, their advantages, and their disadvantages.

Figure 10.1. Training Room Setup

Classroom
- Advantage: Gives participants space to take notes, great for lecture situations
- Disadvantage: Provides minimal interaction among participants

Theater
- Advantage: Allows for large groups to participate
- Disadvantage: Not conducive for sessions that require participants to take notes or do any standing activities

Boardroom
- Advantage: Great for small groups
- Disadvantage: Doesn't work well for group breakout activities; may imply positions of power based on where people sit

U-shape or Horseshoe
- Advantage: Works well in programs that will have discussions or demonstrations
- Disadvantage: Space intensive; not always conducive for group breakout activities

Chevron, Cabaret, or Half Circles
- Advantage: Participants can easily work in small groups
- Disadvantage: Discussion and movement between trainer and participants can be difficult; requires certain table sizes

Preparing the Delivery Team

We prepared the participants for their roles in the pilot. We also need to prepare the trainers. At a minimum, give them trainer or facilitator training and allocate time for them to practice. Buy a half-dozen or so books on how to be a trainer or facilitator that they can read. Here are a few titles I keep on my bookshelf:

- *The Secrets of Facilitation: The SMART Guide to Getting Results with Groups*[1]
- *Extreme Facilitation: Guiding Groups Through Controversy and Complexity*[2]
- *Business Improv: Experiential Learning Exercises to Train Employees to Handle Every Situation with Success*[3]

Also, plan to have backup trainers. Stuff happens, and trainers call in sick or attend to an emergency. Manager onboarding cannot stop. Otherwise, it sends the message that manager onboarding isn't important.

Feedback and Evaluations

Let's talk about evaluations from a program perspective and then discuss it for the pilot. You will want to determine what level of evaluation you will use to measure the manager onboarding program. The most widely used is probably Donald Kirpatrick's four-level training evaluation model.[4]

The Kirkpatrick model encompasses four levels of training evaluation. The ease of gathering the evaluation data and the value of the outcome are inversely related.

Level 1 (Reaction) measures how the participants viewed the training. This is usually done via the evaluation form provided to participants at the end of a session. Sometimes the forms are referred to as "smile sheets." On one level, it's important to gauge how people felt when they left training. However, Level 1 evaluations are often criticized for their inability to measure whether the actual transfer of learning took place.

Level 2 (Learning) evaluates how much attendee knowledge has increased as a result of the training. Participants are tested at the beginning of training and then again at the end. Level 2 evaluations are helpful for showing that the transfer of knowledge took place. The downside is they do not show if the participants' newly acquired knowledge is happening on the job.

Level 3 (Behavior) measures whether the employees have applied the knowledge they learned in training on the job. This evaluation usually occurs via observation and would be measured at some point in the future, like three to six months after training. The upside is that a Level 3 evaluation reveals if the employees are applying their new knowledge in their work. The disadvantage is the length of time it takes to get the results.

Level 4 (Results) assesses the results that are achieved because of the training program. Go back to Chapters 4 and 5, and look at the business reasons for having the program in the first place. A Level 4 evaluation connects the results to the goals of the program. Obviously, this is the best outcome. This is why you sold the program in the first place. But as you can imagine, the results take time and resources.

So Level 1 evaluations are the easiest to collect and the least valuable in terms of outcomes. On the other hand, Level 4 evaluations are the hardest to collect and the most valuable. Each organization will have to decide what makes sense for it and where the organization wants to spend its resources. And keep in mind that if your manager onboarding program has several components, you might want to conduct a Level 1 for one component and a Level 2 or 3 for another.

When it comes to the pilot, you might also want to perform different levels of evaluation. I've been involved in programs in which the trainers stayed in touch with the pilot group for an extended period.

Lastly, when it comes to evaluations, be sure to conduct a debrief with the training delivery team about the session. What did the members think went well? What would they do differently? Is there anything they are uncomfortable with (now that they did it or said it in training)? Also speak to the participants' managers. Elicit their feedback about what happened when the employees returned from training.

Yes, employee evaluations are valuable, but more feedback is needed from supervisors and trainers. This is an organizational program, and all stakeholders need to be comfortable with the program and the content.

After receiving feedback from all stakeholders, then you can make any required modifications to the pilot content.

Program Modifications

Based on the feedback you receive about the pilot, you need to do one of three things:

1. *Make the suggested changes to the program.* In that case, return to Chapter 9 and rework the program based on the feedback.
2. *Plan to incorporate the changes in the future.* There may be a chance that the feedback is good, but maybe adding certain changes are too expensive at the moment. So start a list of improvements you want to make to the program. And—this is an important "and"—go back and communicate to the group that the changes are on the list for a later time. The worst thing you can do is ask for feedback and not do anything with it—or let people think you're not doing anything with it.
3. *Lastly, decide that the change doesn't align with the program.* It's possible the feedback aligns with another company program, and you will add those changes accordingly. If the feedback isn't going to be acted on, it's only fair to let the group know and the reason.

The pilot group plays a major role in training design. It allows the organization to test drive the content. Trainers get a chance to practice delivery. Participant feedback and buy-in are created. Here's a quick recap of how to roll out a pilot group:

Step 1: Select the participants.

Step 2: Cover training logistics with participants and trainers.

Step 3: Give the training team time to practice. And the tools to do the job.

Step 4: Choose an evaluation method that will give you reliable results.

Step 5: Modify the program based on pilot group feedback.

The manager onboarding program is now ready to be implemented in the organization. In the next chapter, we'll discuss tips and resources for delivering a terrific manager onboarding experience.

Chapter 11.

Program Implementation

We've conducted the pilot, and now we're ready to introduce the program to the entire organization. This is the most visible part of the process, and it's important to launch the program with a certain amount of fanfare. A lot of people have been involved during the stages of gaining approval, developing the program, and providing feedback regarding the content. The program has used organizational resources, including employee time and financial resources. And lastly, it's probably been months in the making—from the first conversations to program development to implementation. All of the effort needs to be recognized not only for the individuals who developed the program but for the ones who will be attending for the first time.

There's nothing wrong with letting participants know all the work that has gone into the program. In fact, one of the things to consider is to include a thank-you to everyone who worked on the manager onboarding program in any possible materials (for example, a binder or training guide). If you do so, be sure to double- and triple-check the list, so no one is left out and feelings get hurt.

Years ago, I worked on a huge training project for a cruise line. We didn't get our names in a binder, but the program manager gave each of us a memento for being a part of the development team. The gift was a model ship. It didn't matter if we were internal staff or external consultants: We were a part of the team that brought the program to life. Even though the project happened well over a decade ago, I still have the tiny model ship to this day. Developing a high-profile training program can build a sense of teamwork and camaraderie. Recognizing the effort is the right thing to do.

Participant Logistics

In the last chapter, we talked about logistics for the pilot group. There will be logistics for the regular program as well, and it's possible they will not be the same as those for the pilot. Here are a few considerations.

Attendance. The organization needs to decide when a manager should be scheduled to attend manager onboarding. Chances are it will be when a person becomes a manager (versus beforehand). Remember that manager onboarding and management development are two different things, so it's possible that employees will attend management development and not attend manager onboarding until they officially have a manager role. The question becomes, should people be scheduled for manager onboarding on their first day, during their first week, or within their first month. Organizations must also decide if their department will schedule them for training or if they will automatically be scheduled to attend.

Prerequisites. While in this section we've been talking about the training program portion of onboarding, it's likely that manager onboarding will also have other components like mentoring or management development. The organization will have to decide if managers should take certain components before attending manager onboarding. It will also be necessary to decide the process for new managers being hired from outside the organization.

Welcome/logistics letter. When new managers are scheduled to attend the program, they should receive some sort of welcome to the program that includes an outline of what will happen during the program. That will help new managers prepare their time and help excite them about the learning experience. The letter should also include details like attire, meals, breaks, technology, parking, and room location. Another thing to consider is who the letter should come from. It sounds like a small detail, but I've attended management programs in which the invitation came from the CEO. The company wanted to send the message that the program was important and had the full support of the organization.

Facilitator bio. I'm noticing a larger group of organizations starting to tell participants before training who the facilitator is and to share some information about his or her experience. Of course, there will be introductions during the actual program, but the delivery team has credibility, and participants need to know that. Also, I have to say as a facilitator, it's hard to stand up in front of a group and share your accomplishments. Including a bio allows the organization to share information about facilitators that they might be reluctant to share on their own.

The logistics for the pilot group were unique to that event. It's possible the group was larger or smaller. Maybe it was held in a different location. The logistics for the implementation and regular program should be considered separately.

Time to Think about Program Maintenance

One of the reasons that program implementation and logistics are so important is because of program maintenance. Any time a program or policy or activity is designed and implemented, it must be maintained. I've seen really terrific programs lose their impact because no one thought about how they were going to be maintained.

We've heard that old phrase taken from the movie *Field of Dreams*, "If you build it, they will come." The truth is . . . they won't. It takes more than just creating or building something for people to use it. People have to understand the WIIFM—what's in it for me—before they start to embrace something. Here's an example: A few years ago, I was asked to get involved in the development of an employee onboarding program. The company had built a terrific online repository of information for employees to use, accessible anytime. But employees didn't use it. Why? Well, there were several reasons:

- No one knew it existed.
- It's easier to just walk around the corner and ask someone.
- The system has a lot of information, but it's not updated regularly.
- Information located in one section of the system doesn't match information found in another section.
- And the list goes on.

When we create things, part of the process needs to be establishing a clear understanding of how it will be maintained. I've seen plenty of great things fall to the wayside because no one stopped to consider what happens once they're implemented.

If your job is to build something, consider all the phases. Not just design and creation—but how to implement, communicate, and maintain. Otherwise, all your hard work could be for nothing. As you're getting ready to implement your manager onboarding program, ask the question, "How will we maintain this?"

Review Evaluations Regularly

In the last chapter, we discussed the different levels of program evaluation. At a minimum, you should conduct a Level 1 evaluation. And those evaluations should be summarized and reviewed on a regular basis. It's possible that one isolated comment during a program might not be noteworthy, but if the comment shows up several times over a six-month period, it merits discussion.

Conducting regular reviews allows you to identify trends that will improve the program effectiveness. But be careful about reacting too quickly or before a trend has been identified. I once conducted a regular training program for an organization that asked me to revise the program based on comments received after each class. So after one session they asked me to remove an activity based on that session's evaluations. Next time they asked me to add it back because of new comments received. Needless to say, it was frustrating, not only for me as the facilitator but also because the program lacked consistency. Changes are expected, but too many changes compromise the learning experience. (Besides, this is why the pilot was conducted in the first place—to work out these details.)

Another thing to consider: If you think multiple changes need to be made to the program, conduct another pilot group before introducing Manager Onboarding 2.0 to the organization. There's no rule that says you can have only one pilot group. A secondary benefit of a second pilot group would be that there is a clear indicator of who attended version

1.0 and who attended version 2.0. You can decide if that's important to your organization. It might be—especially in highly regulated industries.

Even if you don't perform a Level 3 evaluation, schedule time to follow up with the three stakeholder groups: facilitators, participants, and managers:

- *Make sure facilitators still have the resources they need.* Find out if they think content needs to be added. In my training programs, I found that I would regularly receive questions about how to effectively implement ideas that participants learned in training. So instead of waiting for the question, I simply added it to the training. Also, if you have multiple facilitators for the same program, give them time to share ideas and learn from each other.
- *Schedule participant conversations at regular intervals to see how they are putting the content to use.* Ask them if there's anything they found particularly useful in the training and if there's anything they wish they would have known earlier. The answers will provide some sense of whether the learning is well timed and valuable.
- *Managers can shed light on how they view the manager onboarding program from a unique perspective.* They can tell you if the program is meeting its goal of making managers productive in an effective and efficient way. That's the program goal we sold to senior management. Managers should be able to see clearly that participation in the program is helping new managers be successful.

Regularly soliciting feedback makes sure the program continues to meet its goals and the content remains relevant. It also helps if you weren't able to implement everything you wanted initially. As the program proves itself, feedback and evaluations can serve as the basis to add other components such as mentoring and coaching.

Maintenance Doesn't Mean Static

Program implementation is the most visible step of the process so far. This is where participants and senior management decide if the manager onboarding program is relevant and valuable. While moving into a program maintenance mode does make things more routine, it also adds a new level of complexity to ensuring that the program is meeting its goals. Implementing your program should include the following steps:

Step 1: Recognize the project team.

Step 2: Make program participation special.

Step 3: Create a process you can maintain.

Step 4: Regularly evaluate program results.

In Chapter 7, we performed an assessment to determine program content, and in this chapter we discussed the possibility of adding new components over time to the manager onboarding program. What topics might be worth consideration? We'll discuss some of the options in the next section.

Part IV:

Manager Onboarding Content

"The biggest mistake companies make is promoting the most technically competent person…and not giving them the tools to do the job."

—*Sharlyn Lauby*

Chapter 12.

Technical (Hard) Skills

The biggest mistake that organizations make is hiring or promoting the most technically competent person into a management role, and then not giving that person the rest of the tools he or she needs to be successful. Yes, technical competence is important, but it's not the only thing. In fact, I do sometimes wonder if one of the reasons that managers are labeled as "micromanagers" is because that's all they know—the technical side. It's what they are most comfortable with, so they are quick to jump into those situations to stay in their comfort zone.

A Case Study in Management

Years ago, I heard a case study that made me realize the importance of knowing more than just technical skills. I often share it with training classes, so I wanted to share it with you. The study examined an incident that took place in August 1949 at Mann Gulch in the Helena National Forest located in Montana (see Figure 12.1).[1]

Mann Gulch lies in west-central Montana and runs into the Missouri River. This area is typified by wet winters and incredibly dry summers. Such was the case in August 1949. The temperature that day was expected to reach 97 degrees. The U.S. Forest Service had put the fire potential at the highest level.

During the previous night, what was reported to be a dry thunderstorm passed through Mann Gulch (Point 1). There were several lightning hits but no precipitation. One lightning strike ignited what was believed to be a small fire (Point 2).

Figure 12.1. The Fire at Mann Gulch

Map by Joel Kimmel. Reproduced with permission from Kathryn Schulz, "The Story That Tore Through the Trees," *New York* magazine, September 9, 2014, http://nymag.com/arts/books/features/mann-gulch-norman-maclean-2014-9.

That afternoon, a relatively small 15-man fire response team was dispatched from nearby Missoula. The leader of the group, Crew Chief Wagner Dodge, had many years of service and was widely known for his technical expertise.

The firefighting crew was relatively young, but they did have experience. Some of the men were professional firefighters, and a couple of them were World War II veterans. This group was selected on the basis of "most rested, ready to go," which was standard practice at the time as people were rotated in and out of firefighting situations. They had never worked as a group before, and many had never worked with Dodge. In fact, it appeared that he didn't even know all of their names.

Shortly after 3:30 in the afternoon, the crew was loaded into an airplane and taken to Mann Gulch.

The aircraft circled several times trying to identify a safe landing zone for the parachuting crew. The men were being bounced around because of stronger-than-expected winds. Dodge and his spotter found what they thought to be a safe landing spot at the northern part of the gulch. By 4:00 that afternoon, the crew had landed in the landing zone (Point 3).

The crew members were more spread out than they had wanted to be because of the unusually strong winds. But by 5:00 all of them were gathered and ready to go. Dodge had already made sure the crew was fed—a standard practice since they may not have the chance before they were done for the day. Shortly after 5:00, Dodge led the group down the gulch where they met up with an advance fire spotter.

There they discovered two significant problems:

1. Their radio was destroyed during the jump, and they had no backup. So they were isolated without communication.
2. They had no map. They made the incorrect assumption that the spotter would have the map.

Dodge led the group toward Point 2 where they waited so that Dodge could scout close to the fire. Here, they discovered the first of their three critical problems: The fire was much worse than the reconnaissance had indicated. The winds were 25-40 mph and had whipped up the fire.

Dodge returned to Point 2 and told the men to head for the mouth of the gorge to use the river as an escape route. He then headed back to the landing zone (Point 3) to get food.

At around 5:30, he caught up with the rest of the crew and led them further down the gulch toward the river. There, they made the second terrible discovery: There was a new, unexpected fire—a consequence of the strong winds—that blocked their escape route (Point 4).

Dodge reversed his direction at approximately 5:45 and told the men to drop their equipment and move as fast as possible up the gorge (Point 4). He knew that you can usually outrun a forest fire. But the unusually dry and windy conditions made that impossible. Here, Dodge made the third terrible discovery: Mann Gulch is part of a transition zone. It's where the forest gives way to prairie grass. The grass was shoulder high, dense, dry, and virtually ready to explode. Dodge estimated they had two minutes before the fire would completely overtake them.

At 5:55, Dodge stopped and lit an escape fire in the prairie grass (Point 5). As the fire expanded, Dodge stepped onto the burnt grass. He motioned for his second in command, Robert Sallee, to enter into the burned-out area. Sallee and Walter Rumsey, the man behind him, refused that order and went over the ridge to the west where they were lucky enough to find a rock slide with no vegetation (Point 6). They survived the fire.

The remaining 13 men headed back up the gulch, passing Dodge and commenting on his bizarre actions. Stating that they had no intention of following Dodge, the remaining crew moved toward the landing zone where the fire overcame them.

Dodge, Sallee, and Rumsey survived the fire. The rest of the firefighters perished. It was the worst firefighting disaster until 1994 when the Storm King fire claimed the lives of 14 firefighters.

If you want to use this story in your training programs, you can add a simple but effective debrief. Ask participants:

1. What mistakes did the Forest Service make? Common responses include poor preparation, misinformation, not conducting team training, and possibly even promoting Dodge in the first place. You can use that response to ask the next question.

2. What mistakes did Dodge make? Participants will mention not having good relationships with the team and failing to communicate with Sallee.

As Norman Maclean recounted in his book about the event, Dodge was good *technically* but inept at building relationships with others. The fire that Dodge started was brilliant and emblematic of his strong technical skills. It was something that the Plains Indians had used for centuries. If Sallee had followed Dodge into the burned-out zone, there's a good chance the rest of the men probably would have followed, and they all would have survived. (Just in case you're wondering, Dodge was ultimately cleared of any culpability in the event.)

This case study demonstrates why technical skills cannot be our only form of expertise as a manager. But I don't want to dismiss technical (or hard) skills completely. There are many moments when they can serve us well.

First off, let's define what are considered to be hard skills. I tend to think of them as skills that are measurable or quantifiable. Examples include typing speed, machine operation, or computer programming—skills for which a person may earn a certificate to indicate proficiency. By contrast, soft skills—which we will cover in the next chapter—are harder to quantify and most often relate to people. Examples are communication, teamwork, collaboration, and listening.

When it comes to hard skills like machine operation and computer programming, those will be determined by your job and industry. But there are a few hard skills that apply to almost every manager position. Managers don't necessarily have to know them to become a manager, and they might not need to know them immediately upon becoming a manager. But at some point, these hard skills will be necessary for a manager's success.

Technology Skills Are a Must-Have

One of the most important hard skills we need in today's business world is computer skills. I believe there's an assumption in organizations that every human being over a certain age understands the Microsoft Office suite. I'm not saying that it's a correct assumption, but I don't remember the last time anyone asked me if I knew how to operate a word processing or spreadsheet program. The assumption is that I know how and that if I don't, I will find out on my own.

The "finding out on my own" part is what's fundamental. Technology is moving at such a rapid pace that managers need to stay on top of current trends. They need to know how to find technology that will help them be more productive and to figure out how to use the technology.

It reminds me of the presentation I heard at the 2013 HR Technology Conference & Exposition. Don Tapscott, co-author of *Paradigm Shift,*[2] was speaking about innovation in a digital age. He used the term "burning platform" as a metaphor in the context of technology and organizational change.

If you're not familiar with the origin of the term, it's based on a story about an oil rig crew member, working in the North Sea off the coast of Scotland. The oil rig had an explosion and the crew member was faced with the decision of dying in the fire or jumping 15 stories into the freezing seas, where his chances of survival were slim at best. He realized that needed to "jump or fry." He jumped. And he survived.

Organizations and individuals are making decisions right now because the cost of staying where they are (that is, the status quo) is greater than the cost of adopting something new. This applies not only to technology but to other aspects of the business as well. It's one of the reasons we're having a conversation about manager onboarding.

While being faced with a dire situation might help managers make much-needed change, this is certainly not ideal decision-making. Ultimately, managers need to figure out how to become "effective adopters." Not everyone has to be an early adopter, but managers certainly don't want to be so late to the party that they can't catch up or keep their teams effective. This applies to organizations as well. Here are five steps that can encourage managers to become effective adopters:

1. *Recognize the trends.* One way to see the next big thing is to notice what employees are talking about. Even if they're talking about what a ridiculous idea something might be, that could be a conversation worth investigating.

2. *Research the trend.* Once a potentially viable trend or idea has been identified, do some homework. With the popularity of bring your own device (BYOD) policies, many organizations allow managers to decide for themselves whether something is good for their productivity. Find out what colleagues are doing and what they claim are the benefits and disadvantages.

3. *Make a commitment to try something new.* If the research indicates the possibility of a win, find a way to test out the new technology or

idea. This goes for the manager and the organization. The manager should give it a try, and the company should support it. Define what will happen and the resources being committed. Also, identify what results or outcomes are expected.

4. *Participate at a high level.* Everyone might be tempted at the first sign of difficulty to give up on the experiment. "I knew this was a waste of time!" Please, resist the urge. Give the experiment your full attention—again, this goes for both the manager and the company. It's possible the benefits will be realized (but not immediately) or an unanticipated benefit will emerge.

5. *Evaluate results.* Even if the decision is made not to move forward, my guess is you will learn a lot from the experiment. For one thing, everyone will be knowledgeable about the topic and aware of trend changes.

Here's an example I find myself talking about a lot. Let's say your organization has hired a new sales manager. During the manager's on-boarding, a conversation starts about social media. You remember a few years ago hearing something about this "trend" called Twitter. On the surface, it looks weird—people talking about cats and bacon 24/7—not worth the company's time.

But the sales manager mentions that in 2015 Twitter had over 300 million active users worldwide, an approximate increase of 20 percent from the year before.[3] Since the conversation, you hear more employees talking about Twitter and even start to see television ads mentioning Twitter. So you decide to investigate. You learn that 67 percent of Twitter users are more likely to buy from the brands they follow on Twitter.[4] Based on that, the company and the sales manager decide to give it a try for 30 days to see what happens. After a month of no recordable sales, the verdict is Twitter is still a waste of time, and the company account is closed.

A few weeks later, a trade publication has an article about distribution tools like Buffer and TweetDeck. The sales manager suggests giving the experiment another try because the new trend addresses some of the challenges raised during the last test run. Now, the company is getting the hang of it and seeing the results it was looking for.

I think we would all agree that managers today need to have excellent technology skills. This includes word processing software, mobile technology, and social media platforms. More importantly, they need to know which technology (that is, devices, software, apps, and more) they should focus on and a process for evaluating their effectiveness. Being an expert in technology that is now irrelevant doesn't benefit anyone.

Process Improvement Applies Everywhere

Organizations use many methodologies for process improvement. They include Six Sigma, lean management, agile management, total quality management, and Kaizen, and the list goes on. I'm not here to debate the pros and cons of each. Depending on your industry, one methodology could be more prevalent than another. The important piece is that the organization has a process improvement methodology and that the organization uses it.

The concept of process improvement is that the organization and its internal processes are doing things properly to be as efficient as possible. It's about increased quality and waste reduction and better resource use. In some organizations, managers might attend a dedicated program to receive a certification in process improvement techniques. Larger organizations might have qualified instructors to teach process improvement certification programs. Smaller organizations could find executive education programs at their local college or university.

On some level, process improvement methodologies have common components. We've talked about many of them already in this book:

1. *Identifying the need for change.* All process improvements start with the realization that change needs to happen. In this situation, the organization realizes that the key to engaging and retaining talent is giving new managers more training and tools.

2. *Assessing the current situation.* This step involves understanding what managers need to know to be successful, what knowledge and skills they have, and how they learn skills in the current environment.

3. *Getting buy-in, support and resources.* Nothing happens in organizations without buy-in, support, and resources. This could be the most time-consuming step in the process, and for some it might involve office politics. But it's necessary.

4. *Create an improvement strategy.* Document the plan for change. Be thorough while allowing for some flexibility. I've never seen a plan that didn't need some tweaking along the way. That's not an excuse for a half-baked plan. It is a reason not to allow analysis paralysis to stop improvements from happening.

5. *Execute the strategy.* After creating the plan, focus on working the plan. If you don't have a copy of the book, *Execution: The Discipline of Getting Things Done* by Larry Bossidy and Ram Charan,[5] consider getting a copy. It's all about how to turn plans into action.

Process improvement methodologies can benefit any industry and any business. Managers can use the principles of process improvement in many aspects of their jobs. It's a technical skill that managers need to have and possibly even all *employees* (but that's another book).

Project Management Skills Can Be Used Every Day

It could be said that much of the work we do is managing projects. Maybe it's a small project that takes a half day. Or possibly it's a big project that takes well over a year. Either way, we're managing various projects all the time, and we use the same set of skills for each project.

Like process improvement, project management skills can be taught in a formal training environment. They can also be learned in a more modular way. Each skill is learned independently, then the training turns to how to use them together. And like process improvement, we've mentioned some of these skills already in this book.

Project scope. This can be viewed as the project goal (that is, what is the project trying to accomplish?). Probably the most well-known term in project management is "scope creep," meaning that additional objectives are added to the goal, often without additional resources. It can have a negative impact on the final outcomes of the project. It's also something that we have to be concerned about with the development of manager onboarding. Be careful that the project doesn't get too big or so watered down with topics that it loses its effectiveness.

Project plan. Like a SMART (specific, measurable, actionable, responsible, time-bound) plan or a process improvement plan, this is the working document that everyone will work from. It contains the project scope, the results to be accomplished, the individuals responsible, and deadline dates. It's monitored, updated, and distributed regularly.

Schedules. The two most common project management scheduling tools are Gantt charts and PERT charts. Gantt charts were developed in the early 1900s by Henry Gantt. They are a type of bar chart that illustrates the start and completion dates for the tasks in a project. PERT stands for Program Evaluation Review Technique, and the U.S. Navy developed it in the 1950s. A PERT chart shows the tasks that need to be completed and their relationship to other tasks in the project.[6]

Budgets. Back in Chapter 6, we talked about putting a budget together for the manager onboarding program. Every project has a budget. Managers must know how to read budgets, create budgets, monitor budgets, and, finally, adjust budgets.

Communication. I would categorize communication skills as a soft skill, which we'll cover in more detail in the next chapter. Project management involves communication skills. Project team members need to know how to lead a meeting, work as a team, manage conflict, make decisions, and communicate change. All of the skills above involve communication. For example, you cannot build a budget without communication. Or a schedule. Or a project plan. Or a project scope.

New managers are often asked to participate on committees, task forces, and project teams on which they've never served before. Having skills in project management, process improvement, and technology can help them feel comfortable with the new assignment. Feeling comfortable translates into engagement and, ultimately, success.

As I mentioned, in the next chapter, we'll cover soft skills. While they are more difficult to quantify, soft skills are equally as important. And maybe because they are a challenge to measure, they can be more difficult to build into training programs.

Chapter 13.

Management (Soft) Skills

In the last chapter, we talked about hard skills. This chapter focuses on the other side of the equation—soft skills. They're the hard-to-measure skills that, in addition to hard skills, we need to be successful. Sometimes they are referred to as "people skills."

In thinking about all of the different soft skills that should be considered in a manager onboarding program, I thought the best standard could be taken from the Society for Human Resource Management (SHRM) Competency Model (see Figure 13.1).

Figure 13.1. The 9 Critical Competencies

Here's my logic: This is the competency model for HR career success. It's been validated. It contains technical (hard) skills and people (soft) skills. And much of our role as HR professionals is to help managers with the human resource aspects of their departments or span of control. So using the SHRM Competency Model as a guide makes a lot of sense.

The challenging part when it comes to soft skills will be deciding which soft skills should be included in the organization's new-hire onboarding for all employees, general training offering, management development program, or manager onboarding program.[1] All the soft skills in this chapter are relevant. It will be up to each organization to decide who should receive training and when. Industry could drive that. It could also be driven by the goals of the organization.

So for this chapter, let's talk about the various soft skills that could be incorporated into a manager onboarding program along with their advantages and disadvantages.

Communication Skills

An employer survey conducted by Hart Research Associates showed that 93 percent of employers consider good communication more important than a college graduate's major.[2] SIS International Research discovered that 70 percent of small to midsize businesses claim that ineffective communication is a costly problem.[3] As an example, the researchers found that a business with 100 employees spends an average downtime of 17 hours per week clarifying communications, estimating the cost as $528,443 annually.

I know, communication skills seems like an obvious inclusion for a manager onboarding program. But I think there are communication skills that every employee would benefit from—for example, listening skills. Everyone can use active listening techniques, so that skill might be better covered in a general employee training program.

Then, managers need to be exposed to listening skills specifically for the responsibilities they have as managers. As we will discuss later, activities such as employee coaching, networking, and decision-making, are topics to consider for a manager onboarding program so listening skills can be included in other manager-specific training programs.

Three areas in which manager-specific communication skills would be valuable are (a) written communication skills, (b) presentation skills, and (c) personality or behavioral assessments.

One of the first things that happens when someone becomes a manager is the expectation that he or she will write memos, e-mails, and reports. Managers will use their writing skills in project reports, business proposals, policies, procedures, employee reviews, and possibly employee discipline.

We're not talking about grammar here; although if you have managers that need some grammar lessons, maybe refer them to a business writing course. The type of writing training we're talking about here is effectiveness. Managers need to know how to effectively and efficiently communicate their thoughts on paper. I had a boss once who wanted to see my ideas in writing before discussing them with me. Maybe it was a quirk in his personality, but it helped me learn how to write. I needed to be thorough yet brief. I found that, by the time we discussed my idea, I had completely researched the topic, thought of all the contingencies, and could quickly articulate my point of view.

If managers know how to write but they struggle with the format, the organization can create templates for memos, reports, and other types of documents that will standardize formatting. That could be a benefit for the entire organization.

Managers who struggle with finding the right words to say in employee communications might find "Phrases" books helpful. HR could put together a manager library of reference materials that would help every manager all year long.[4]

While organizations can provide managers with several writing tools, I still can envision a portion of manager onboarding being dedicated to how to communicate effectively and efficiently in writing within the organization.

After the expectation that managers can write, the next expectation is that they can speak (as in delivering a presentation). Ideally, managers should attend a train-the-trainer (T3) program to learn the best way to develop and deliver a presentation. However, T3 programs are long, so at the point a manager needs it, the program isn't always an option.

For that reason, manager onboarding programs need to find a way for new managers to become comfortable speaking in front of people, in a safe environment. It could be doing a five-minute presentation on a technical skill they are comfortable with. Or a short lunch-and-learn session of a small group of employees. The last thing new managers should be subjected to is having their first presentation be a long, multimedia session on a topic that's somewhat new to both them and the senior management team that will result in either a big win or an epic loss.

Manager onboarding programs can build in opportunities for small presentations until organizations are able to schedule the new manager for a formal T3 program. Depending on the size of your organization, T3 might be something offered on a regular basis. I've worked for companies that held sessions a couple of times a year; we didn't have the need to conduct more sessions than that. There are also reputable companies offering T3 courses to the public.

The third area for manager-specific communication is personality or behavioral assessments. I'll cover assessments more in Chapter 16. There are many assessments on the market, and I'm not here to promote one over another. Your organization might have one you're already using, and you love it. My point about assessments is that new managers need to learn how to communicate with others. Much of their success is contingent on their ability to communicate with employees, their peers, and their boss. To communicate effectively with others, you need to understand your audience. The best way to start learning how to read your audience is by becoming self-aware. The right assessment can be valuable in helping managers in their journey of self-awareness.

Two things to always remember when talking about assessments: First, whatever assessment you choose, make sure it is valid and reliable for the way you are using it. Second, train the individuals who will be administering and discussing assessment results on the specifics of the assessment.

High Performers Have High Emotional Intelligence

Emotional intelligence is the capacity to be aware of, control, express, and handle interpersonal relationships with empathy.[5] According to a survey conducted by TalentSmart, emotional intelligence is the strongest predictor of performance.[5]

This is why Glassdoor, one of the fastest-growing job and career websites in the U.S., includes emotional intelligence in its manager onboarding program. I had the chance to speak with Kerry Schlatter, head of the employee experience at Glassdoor, to learn more about the company's onboarding programs.

Kerry, what does your new-hire onboarding program look like?
[Schlatter] Our day-long onboarding program starts with an overview of Glassdoor, and then, throughout the day, new hires are immersed in several elements of Glassdoor including product overviews, a breakdown of our benefits offerings and employee wellness initiatives, and of course, administrative overviews.

Our newest addition, the Culture & Values Segment, has been a big hit as employees are able to understand exactly who we are, and who we are not. We end this informative first day with a scavenger-hunt-style tour of the office where new hires discover fun quirks of Glassdoor like the nap room, the PR dog, and the best places to find snacks.

Do you have any components that are specific for management? If so, what are they?
[Schlatter] Something that started as management training and moved to mandatory for all employees is our "Emotional Intelligence" training. We work with a third party to provide this training throughout the year, and our internal head coach, Mariah DeLeon, provides leadership workshops and emotional trainings for all employees to further this training. The purpose of this is to prepare employees to have difficult conversations constructively and with compassion for one another.

A separate mandatory management training includes discussion on how to approve time for hourly employees, onboard employees, create a performance improvement plan, off-board employees, and whom to alert when any changes occur on their teams.

How long did it take to design your onboarding program?
[Schlatter] It is an ongoing process. Glassdoor is built on the notion that everyone is entitled to his or her opinion, and we look to our employees for ideas on how we can change and continue to improve these programs. Initially, HR put together the program and worked with recruiting, finance, and IT to make sure it was efficient and all-encompassing. Today, we seek feedback from all employees at Glassdoor as we constantly look for ways to improve.

Was there anything that surprised you during the design—maybe feedback you didn't expect or results beyond what you initially anticipated?
[Schlatter] We were inclusive in the process and had several sprints before finalizing and launching, so I wouldn't say I was surprised by feedback. Along the way I've been more surprised to see how different people experience the program differently. What one employee finds incredibly engaging and exciting, another can have a very hard time participating in. For example, our emotional intelligence training isn't something everyone is thrilled about going into. However, once it's done, I'm surprised how many people come back to tell me how valuable they found it, especially those who were skeptical to begin with.

What kind of results do you measure?
[Schlatter] We conduct frequent employee surveys to gather feedback on specific events like All Hands meetings, review cycles, and onboarding. We also host "Getting to Know You" meetings with the head of HR and 90-day check-ins with new hires. We also closely watch our app-to-hire ratios, cost-of-hire, cost-of-applicant, and attrition rates. Not to mention, we use Glassdoor to monitor employee satisfaction.

Consultation Skills

Back in Chapter 3, we discussed consultation skills in the context of the need for manager onboarding. It's likely those three steps we outlined—establish collaborative relationships, pay attention to business problems, and solve problems so they stay solved—will be necessary for every manager to learn. I'm not sure, though, that manager onboarding is the place for them.

Learning to collaborate is an important skill typically introduced during team development. Please notice that I didn't say "team building." Team development is about the team members gaining specific competencies that will help them become productive members of the team—any team. Team building is about role clarification, goal setting, and interpersonal relationships with a specific team. Both are valuable. But ideally, every organization should want every employee to know how to collaborate.

Problem solving can take on many different forms within an organization. I can see giving all employees a basic problem-solving model and managers a more in-depth view of the same model—and possibly an even deeper dive for certain positions, such as engineering. So depending on the organization and industry, problem solving could be a topic about which manager-specific content is developed. Like presentation skills, it might not be something that a new manager needs exposure to right away but something that gets scheduled within the manager's first 30 or 60 days in the position.

Many organizational cultures still view managers as being the problem solvers. In addition, many employees feel it's their manager's job to solve their problems. Though that perception may be incorrect, it is a perception that managers must deal with. Therefore, it would not be helpful to new managers to prevent them from learning all they can about problem solving.

Another aspect of problem solving that managers are often associated with is conflict management. When conflict exists among employees, many in the organization look to the manager to help resolve the conflict. While employees should ideally be able to resolve their own conflicts, unresolved or escalating conflict can affect team dynamics, departments, and results. Managers might have no choice but to step in and facilitate a resolution.

Even if the organization offers a general conflict management program for all employees, it would be beneficial to have a program focused on the types of problems and conflict that managers are asked to resolve. Although fixing a broken piece of equipment and redesigning a broken process are both problems, they have nuances that differ. Manager onboarding programs could address those differences.

This is also a good time to talk about situations in which a manager is hired from the outside or promoted from within *and* the company knows there's a problem the manager will need to solve. I'm reminded of a story from early in my career.

"Plan more parties." That's what the company leaders said when I asked them the biggest challenge facing human resources.

I was interviewing for a director-level position. During the conversation, I asked what the biggest challenge was facing the company's HR department. Everyone told me the same thing: Employee morale is low, and we need to have more employee parties. So, I thought, I can do parties. In fact, I plan great parties. I'm the one you need. And several interviews later, I was offered the job.

Once I started work, I noticed something odd. I would be in my office, working away, and when employees came into HR . . . they came to my office. No one else's office. Only my office. It didn't matter what the request was for.

Employee with an insurance question—my office.

Supervisor wanting to talk about promoting an employee—my office.

Manager to discuss employee cafeteria ideas—my office.

After two weeks of this, my boss called me in to ask me how I was settling in. Not sure how he would take my answer, I said "You guys told me that what was needed around here were more parties. If I didn't know any better, I'd say there's a problem in the human resources department."

His reply? "I'm glad you figured it out."

He went on to explain that human resources "didn't feel warm." Not that the thermostat was broken, but that the people working in the department weren't friendly and helpful. They viewed employees as a disruption to their day instead of a customer within the organization.

Ultimately, HR had to change. And after several months, and unfortunately, a few personnel changes, employees were using the entire HR department. Not just one person.

To finish the story, I remember him coming to the HR office a few months later, faking a glance at the thermostat and saying, "It's warm in here." We all smiled.

I was lucky. I figured it out. The question is, how many managers are put in the same position, and they *don't* figure it out? Problem solving should be a part of manager onboarding.

Leadership Skills

Remember at the beginning of the book when we defined leadership as the ability to influence others? This is why. Leadership exists at every level of the organization. Honestly, every employee should receive leadership skills training. The organization would benefit from it; I can't see any downside to it. There are plenty of components to manager onboarding. Leadership training should be separate and thought of in a holistic way instead of thinking that managers should be the only people to benefit from it.

Employees want to work for social leaders

According to LinkedIn, managers are starting to realize that being active on social media is essential to their role. LinkedIn cited a study that indicates 76 percent of managers say they would rather work for a social CEO.

To help managers become more social-media savvy, LinkedIn published *Executive Playbook: 12 Steps to Become a Social Leader.*[7] This e-book contains tips and strategies for using social media to improve relationships with customers, employees, and peers. The tips range from empowering your team to offering an authentic voice to your company brand.

Ethics

Ethics training should be a part of manager onboarding, even if you're in an industry that's heavily regulated with highly defined ethics policies that all employees are required to sign off on. Managers are typically involved in purchasing activities, budgets, and vendor contracts. From an employee perspective, managers are involved in hiring, pay increases, and, sometimes, employee investigations. These activities could be new responsibilities, and with them come new ethics standards.

Ethics could be considered one of those topics covered on day one with a new manager. If new-manager orientation occurs on the first day, then it might be included there. Or if the organization has an onboarding portal, manager ethics might be a video that new managers are required to view. The good news is that there's some flexibility on how manager ethics is built into the program. But the training definitely should be in the program. It would be a terrible thing for new managers to commit an ethics violation because they didn't know the law or understand the culture. Such an act would damage their personal and professional credibility, which would ultimately affect job performance.

Relationship Management

The SHRM Competency Model defines "relationship management" as "the ability to manage interaction, to provide service, and to support the organization."[8] The skills we've talked about so far—communications, consulting, leadership, and ethics—all factor into relationship management. But there are two manager-specific topics we haven't covered so far that directly align with relationship management.

The first is coaching. *Managers are coaches.* Let me say that again. Managers are coaches. They coach employees to perform better. They coach employees to correct bad behavior. Successful managers spend the majority of their time coaching employees. While organizations can teach the mechanics of coaching in a management development program, it's hard to refine the skill without actually getting to practice coaching. So employee coaching is one of those topics that start in a management development program and transition to manager onboarding.

In fact, something to consider when thinking about how managers can perfect their employee coaching skills is the various ways to offer the content. It could be introduced in a management development program and videotaped. A refresher video could then be made available to all managers so they could view the video before a coaching conversation. Moreover, HR and IT could develop job aids for managers to keep on their mobile devices—these would be especially valuable for managers who have virtual teams.

To help new managers become comfortable having coaching conversations, assign them a buddy or mentor. The role of the buddy is to help the new manager feel at ease with the process and delivery of performance feedback, not to make decisions about employee performance.

The second topic that aligns with relationship management is networking. Google defines it as "interacting with other people to exchange information and develop contacts." As business professionals, we must realize that networking is essential to our career success and not something that is done only when one is looking for a new job. We can learn from networking. Our contacts can expose us to new ideas; they can share information with us and keep us from having to recreate forms or processes that have already been proven somewhere else. But for networking to happen, it must have senior management's support and guidance.

Organizations can give networking tips and resources to new managers throughout their onboarding program. Books such as *Never Eat Alone* can be included in a manager library.[9] But the best way to learn networking is by doing it. That means going to events and meeting people.

You'll notice in both of these topics—networking and coaching—there's the opportunity to bring a buddy or mentor into the program. We'll explore this idea in Chapter 18. For right now, keep in mind that having positive working relationships is necessary for managers. And the best way to learn how to build positive working relationships is by participating in relationship-building activities. Books and workshops are good, but they will take the conversation only so far.

Critical Evaluation

Critical evaluation skills are the ability to understand and interpret relevant data. They play a role in problem solving but also in the daily monitoring of information. The first piece of critical evaluation I call "curation." It's the ability to find relevant, accurate data and information. To offer some perspective, according to Gwava, an archiving and security company, here is the amount of data created on the Internet each day:[10]

- 500 million Tweets sent, and another 40 million shared.
- 4 million hours of video on YouTube.
- 4.3 billion Facebook posts 5.75 billion likes.
- 6 billion Google searches.
- 205 billion e-mails.

Even if these numbers are slightly inflated, the bottom line is that we are overwhelmed with information on the Web. A simple Google search for "management" will return 2.57 billion (yes with a "b") responses. Asking a manager to "do a little research" isn't what it used to be.

Managers are not alone in facing this issue. If employees are being asked to research information, they're in the same situation. Offering training on how to search and identify reliable information will benefit the whole organization. This is also a place where having excellent technology skills is valuable.

But there's a second piece to critical evaluation—interpreting the data. This is the component that might be specific to managers. Many people inside the organization could be responsible for gathering data, but managers *interpret* the data.

Like the topics we mentioned under relationship management, learning how to interpret data gets easier the more you do it. Creating case studies for managers to read and discuss may be an excellent way to have managers practice their decision-making skills in a safe environment.

Decision-making is the other soft skill I associate with critical evaluation. After the data are gathered and interpreted, decisions are made. Even if the decision is "we don't need to make a decision right now"—that's a decision. If your business is often faced with what you would categorize as tough calls about the operation, giving new managers a chance to practice making those decisions in a simulated work environment could be valuable. Not to mention helping to build the manager's confidence when the time comes to really make the call. Just in case you're wondering what type of situation could be used as a case study, here's one that comes to mind for me.

When I worked at the airline, I was a part of the emergency response team. On a regular basis, we participated in emergency drills (that is, simulations), where we had an aircraft emergency that we needed to respond to. You hope that you never have to use that training. Unfortunately, we had to use it. I cannot begin to tell you how grateful I am that I was able to practice in a safe environment how to handle a disaster.

New managers are often given additional responsibilities such as becoming a member of the emergency response team. Their organizations need to supply them with the tools to do those jobs well. It's possible that new managers are not assigned additional roles on day one, but when they receive those extra responsibilities, they need to be provided a plan to learn the skills.

An example for me was when I moved to South Florida; I wasn't a member of the hurricane response committee at first. But a few months into my role (and a couple of months before hurricane season started), I was asked to participate. It was then I received the training I needed.

When we think about both soft and hard skills, the truth is, these skills work together. Often the way we initially impress others is with our technical expertise. Our hard skills open doors for us and create opportunities for people to listen to what we have to say. But it's our people skills that allow us to convince others. The soft skills keep the door open for us to walk into the office of our boss or a colleague and say, "Let me run this idea by you."

A manager with loads of technical skills and few people skills will struggle to make things happen. A manager with terrific soft skills and no hard skills will struggle to earn respect from people who know the work. Being a successful manager means having both.

When someone becomes a manager, his or her responsibilities increase. There will be stressful times. Managers need to know how to take care of themselves. Stressed-out managers will only stress out their teams. In the next chapter, we'll talk about well-being tips for managers.

Chapter 14.

Well-Being

Today's workplaces are fast-paced and competitive because those characteristics are needed to be successful in the business world, and companies want to be as efficient as possible. But organizations must be careful that they aren't losing sight of the big picture when it comes to the way they treat employees.

As companies operate full steam ahead, employees are being asked to do more work with fewer resources and little or no support—and it's often overwhelming. They're attempting to manage multiple projects and priorities, leaving them distracted and unable to fully connect at work or home. They're tethered to their devices 24/7/365, answering e-mails in the middle of the night, or cutting back on quality family time to crank out a little more work. They're constantly "on" and in "response mode" with limited time for themselves—meaning they're frequently operating right on the edge of burnout.

Burnout goes hand in hand with disengagement, a real threat to organizations everywhere. With 68 percent of employees *disengaged* at work, tuned-out employees cost U.S. businesses $450-$550 billion, according to Gallup.[1] Let's put this in perspective: If the U.S. labor force has 150 million people, 68 percent (102 million!) are disengaged. That translates to as much as $5,393 per disengaged employee per year. So, if you have 500 employees working in your organization, the impact of disengagement can potentially be in the neighborhood of $1.8 million per year! We talk regularly about HR impacting the organization's bottom line. HR's role in hiring, onboarding, and developing managers reduces the effects of disengagement and increases profitability.

As employees struggle to manage demands on their time and attention, they're feeling increasingly frazzled and putting their well-being last on their list of priorities. New managers must be provided the tools to help employees prevent burnout and practice well-being. It starts with managers understanding how to do that for themselves.

Notice we're talking about well-being and not just wellness, which often focuses only on physical health. Well-being takes a holistic view and involves five major components:

1. *Having a purpose:* Liking what you do each day both in your personal and professional life and being motivated to achieve your goals.
2. *Receiving social support:* Having supportive relationships and love in your life. This also relates to having friends at work.
3. *Being financially literate:* Managing your economic life (for example, budget, savings, investments) to reduce stress and increase security.
4. *Feeling a sense of community:* Liking where you live, feeling safe, and having pride in your community.
5. *Maintaining physical wellness:* Focusing on good health and having enough energy to accomplish things daily.

While some components of well-being may seem a little fluffy at first glance, these areas have a real impact on employees. Research conducted by the Society for Human Resource Management (SHRM) indicates that employees' financial stress is a concern for HR professionals. Sixty-one percent of respondents said financial stress has "some impact" on work performance, while another 22 percent conceded it's a "large impact."[2]

When employees can't make time for their healthy habits and goals, their performance is affected. That, in turn, affects the business. For example, employees who don't get enough sleep are 32 percent less productive.[3] Reversely, when employees maintain healthy habits, it positively affects your company: Employees who regularly exercise during their workday achieve a cognitive uplift of 23 percent, according to the *International Journal of Workplace Health Management.*[4]

Disengaged employees hit your organization hard, and it goes beyond the impact of low employee morale. The attitudes and emotions of employees can influence sales, customer service, and innovation. Employee disengagement also has a huge impact on unscheduled absenteeism, which can range from $2,600 to $3,600 per employee per year.[5]

But simply reducing or eliminating disengagement isn't enough. Creating a happier, healthier, more productive workforce is crucial. Organizations can and should consider well-being programs for their entire workforce. But if managers do not support employee well-being programs on a daily basis, it will have an impact on their success.

That's why manager onboarding needs to include some consideration for well-being. First, no company wants one of its new managers to burn out after making the investment in their success. And second, no organization wants stressed-out managers to hurt the rest of their department.

One of the first ways to help managers keep well-being in perspective is with proper goal setting.

3 Types of Goals

Back in Chapter 8, we talked about goals from an instructional design perspective. Because goals are such an important part of what we do in business, I think it's worth spending more time on goals . . . but this time from an individual perspective.

Regularly in business, we reflect on the goals we've accomplished and start to think about the things we would like to do in the future. But goals are tricky. Set a bad goal, and you could end up wasting time and energy. Set a wrong goal, and you could end up in a situation you didn't want.

For instance, let's say I set a goal to learn how to code. There's nothing wrong with coding, right? Correct. But if I'm not looking to become a full-time coder, I might want to make sure that this goal doesn't take up all of my time, preventing me from having goals related to my full-time occupation.

To make sure that managers set relevant goals, it's important to help them understand what goals are and how they differ from objectives. Often the terms "goals" and "objectives" are used interchangeably. While they are related, they're *not* the same thing.

Goals are long-term achievements. They are usually focused on the future and don't include actual steps to accomplish the goal. For example, a company might say it has a goal "to be number one in customer satisfaction." That's the goal. But it doesn't outline how the goal will be accomplished.

Objectives are specific achievements to help you reach the goal. Typically, they are measurable and have a timeline. If we use the goal example above, an objective might be "to improve customer satisfaction scores by 5 points each quarter."

Using my previous example of learning how to code, here's an illustration of a goal and an objective:

Goal: "I want to learn how to code well enough to attend a hackathon." There's no way I'm going to learn coding overnight, so it's a long-term goal. It's future focused and doesn't have any specific steps on how I plan to achieve the goal.

Objective: "I'm going to download the Hopscotch app to my iPad and complete one activity a day." This is specific—download an app and complete one activity a day. (By the way—if you have a secret goal like me to learn about coding, check out the Hopscotch app. It's fun for adults and kids.)

Knowing the difference between goals and objectives will help you develop achievable goals, which is key in managing your work, your time, and your stress levels. Now comes the fun part, actually thinking about and establishing your goals. There are three types of goals: based on time, focus, and topic.

1. Time goals are the ones we refer to as short term or long term. An example would be having a short-term goal of learning how to make a roux with a long-term goal of learning how to make gumbo.

2. Focus goals remind me of a BHAG (big hairy audacious goal). It's the one thing that is driving the majority of decisions. For instance, I have a goal to write a book. Big goal. It was a huge endeavor and affected many of my personal and professional decisions.

3. Topic-based goals include personal, professional, career, and financial. Maybe you have a goal to save a certain amount of money.

Or to complete a leadership development program. These are goals that are meaningful in a certain aspect of our life.

Time, focus, and topic goals are not mutually exclusive. We can have short-term financial goals, long-term career goals, and a personal BHAG. After establishing a goal, you have to create a plan to make those goals happen. Think of the plan as creating a series of objectives that will ultimately allow you to accomplish the goal. I'm a big fan of using SMART plans to achieve goals. SMART is an acronym.

- *Specific:* What is the specific goal you're trying to accomplish? Be specific!
- *Measurable:* How can you measure your success? Think about how you will know when you've accomplished the goal.
- *Actionable:* What are the actionable steps (aka objectives) needed to achieve the goal? Break the goal into smaller steps. List every step.
- *Responsible:* Who are the people that must support this goal? If you need the support of your manager, co-workers, friends, or family, make note of it here.
- *Time-bound:* When do you want to achieve the goal?

Whenever I have a goal, I outline it on a sheet of paper and post it on my office wall. That way it's staring me in the face every day. Having a written plan helps me achieve my goals. You can also keep a SMART plan online. The important part is setting the goal, creating the plan, and holding yourself accountable for achieving the goal. (Note: You can keep your project plan for developing a manager onboarding program in a SMART plan format.)

Because goal setting is a frequently used term in business, we need to make sure managers know what goals are and how to create them and manage them successfully. They will be responsible for their own goals as well as the goals of their teams. Goal setting is a core function of business success. We can't move forward without goals. Small goals lead to big accomplishments. Short-term goals create long-term achievements. Professional goals can help us realize our personal goals.

What to Do When You Don't Accomplish Your Goals

Goals can help us build confidence, learn new things, and manage massive amounts of work. Which is why we also need to help managers understand how to manage setbacks and failure.

Let's face it: We don't always achieve our goals. If there's a silver lining to not accomplishing your goals, it's this—today's society has embraced the failure concept. What I mean by that is, we are much more receptive to having business conversations about failure. Case in point, basketball star Michael Jordan has a famous quote about failure: "I've missed more than 9,000 shots in my career. I've lost almost 300 games. 26 times, I've been trusted to take the game-winning shot and missed. I've failed over and over and over again in my life. And this is why I succeed." [6]

Jordan isn't the only one. Sara Blakely, Ted Turner, Jack Welch, and Oprah Winfrey have all talked about the benefits of failure. Now, I don't want to say that not achieving a goal is always acceptable and embraced. But on some level, it's okay, provided that you learn from it. When you don't have success with your goals, it's your responsibility to figure out the reason.

In thinking about the reasons we don't accomplish our goals, I break them down into two categories: factors you can control and factors you can't control. Both factors have similarities. For example, let's say I've set a goal to complete a leadership development course. It's on my performance appraisal as one of the professional development items I need to accomplish. The course takes 12 weeks and is offered every quarter by the HR department.

One of the reasons that I might not accomplish this goal is time. I decide that Q3 or Q4 would be a perfect time to take the program. So I've taken Q1 and Q2 out as an option—factors I can control. In Q3, I find out the course is completely booked—a factor I cannot control. So I sign up for Q4. Then my manager gives me a high-profile project to work on and suggests that I postpone participating in the course—another factor outside of my control.

So in this example, time—both in terms of my planning and the company's priorities—contributed to not achieving the goal. What's important to note in this example is that both the company and I had a role in the goal not being accomplished. It would be unfair of the company to penalize me for not achieving its goals since my manager suggested that I not take the Q4 program. And it would be unfair of me to blame the company because I decided to wait until Q4 to sign up.

Once you've figured out the reason(s) that the goal wasn't accomplished, now the tough questions begin. You have to decide if this is still a goal and, if so, if you have to recommit to it. Here are some questions to ask:

- Do I still need to and/or want to accomplish this goal?
- Does the goal need to be redefined in some way?
- Do I have all the resources I need to accomplish this goal?
- What would happen if I did not accomplish this goal a second time?

It's possible after you answer these questions that the answer will be "No, that goal doesn't matter anymore." And that's perfectly acceptable. People and companies, as well as their respective needs, change all the time. What's key is that the parties involved analyze the situation, give their honest feedback, and reach a satisfactory conclusion.

Abandoning a goal takes a lot of guts. If that's the case—the goal will not be pursued again—then everyone invested in that goal needs to understand why. They also need to be allowed to let it go. One of the biggest challenges with failed goals is that they can linger around and stifle future productivity.

On the other hand, if the goal is still important and needs to be accomplished, then all the stakeholders need to recommit. They need to acknowledge the reasons the goal didn't happen the first time and take ownership for those circumstances and for the new goal.

Not accomplishing goals isn't a moment for passing blame. It's a time for reflection and regrouping. It's how people use that time that will ultimately decide success.

Another reason we don't accomplish our goals is distractions. We're human, and we will get distracted. The key to overcoming distractions is staying focused. And managers can play a big role in helping employees stay focused. I had the privilege of interviewing Daniel Goleman, author of the *New York Times* bestseller *Emotional Intelligence*, for my blog, *HR Bartender*.[7] He talked about managers having different kinds of focus.

Leaders who get good results contribute immensely to the bottom line of a company. There are three kinds of focus every high-performance leader needs:

- ○ Inner focus to lead themselves;
- ○ Focus on others, to influence and motivate the people they lead; and
- ○ Focus on the large systems that their company operates in, from the economy and the culture to the natural environment.

Understanding how these are shifting allows a leader to generate effective strategy. Leaders deficient in any one of these three will either be rudderless, clueless, or blindsided.

As technology continues to play a larger role in our personal and professional lives, discussions surrounding the concept of focus will become more frequent. I see many of my friends and colleagues have taken a hiatus or left social platforms because of the distractions. They use terms like "filtering out the noise" or "taking a digital vacation." But the truth is, not all of us can simply take a tech hiatus. And we can't allow our managers to simply fall off the grid for a while. Managers need to find ways to manage technology, get the most out of it, and remain focused.

Signal-to-Noise Ratio

There's a measure in science called the signal-to-noise ratio (abbreviated SNR or S/N). It compares a signal to the level of background noise. In our technology-driven world, it has also come to mean the ratio of useful information to irrelevant data. For example, you might hear that a social media platform has a lot of noise, meaning it contains more worthless data and less valuable conversation than other platforms.

We briefly mentioned the idea of curation in Chapter 13, under the section on critical evaluation. If you're looking for a way to bring the concept of curation into training and learning, here's a three-step approach I learned about from Fujitsu Laboratories.

1. *Search:* Learners decide the topics they want to explore, search for relevant sources, and select content.
2. *Synthesize:* Learners analyze the content and synthesize it by adding their point of view or context.
3. *Share:* Learners share their curated materials and comments with others and receive curated content from others.

Managers follow this approach when they send their teams information they've come across. We see it in the e-mails: "Hey team, check out this article!" or "Here's something I heard about during a conference." The goal for managers and employees is to make sure the information they are curating is relevant and rises above all the noise.

Another way that managers can work on staying focused is by practicing mindfulness. It's defined as the discipline of maintaining awareness of thoughts, feelings, and the surrounding environment. It also involves acceptance, meaning that we don't judge the things we're becoming aware of. Organizational development and effectiveness consultant Elad Levinson is a practitioner of mindfulness and shared his thoughts on how mindfulness has benefited him and his career:[8]

I think of meditation as mind and emotional intelligence training. There are quite subtle but exceptional outcomes from mindfulness training that are valuable for any leader. According to my peers and my staff, mindfulness training has made me:

- Less reactive and more likely to listen carefully to others' perspectives—especially when they are directly in conflict with my own intentions or assumptions. I am able to consider that I might be wrong or need to be inclusive of views that challenge my own.
- Intent on generating and cultivating goodwill with my peers, staff, and stakeholders. I tend to know how to incline

my thinking and actions so that it is in line with my intent to do well in speech or action.

○ Better able to investigate myself. I am extremely curious and you will know this if you are short on time and listening to my latest curiosity or passion-driven exploration! I am aware of so much more of my personality that used to be quite unconscious—and perhaps motivating—but not particularly skillful. My curious nature extends now to understand my drives and motives, and prevents me from mindlessly reacting.

○ Insightful. Insight seems to be an important skill that is developed by mind training. I can see into problems and decision-making processes that in the past I might have ignored or been mindless about.

○ Symbiotic. I know that my newfound authentic interest in others' perspectives leads them to trust me and work more collaboratively with me. I am not a threat to their intentions and desires since I am committed to being inclusive and cooperative when it is appropriate.

Before dismissing mindfulness training as being a little too demonstrative for your organization, consider this: Mindfulness training can help managers become more productive because they can understand themselves better, listen more effectively, respond more intently, solve problems at a higher level, and be more empathic. These are all things that can lead to higher levels of employee engagement.

There's one other thing that mindfulness can do: help managers figure out their flow. Mihaly Csikszentmihalyi developed the term "flow" as a result of his interviews with people who described their absorption in their work as being so natural and fluid that it carried them along like water, without conscious effort and with tremendous focus.[9]

I had the opportunity to speak with Catherine Flavin, managing partner at Thrive Leadership, about Csikszentmihalyi's work and the concept of flow on HR Bartender.[10] I'm publishing a few excerpts of the interview here. I think flow is important to managers being able to enjoy and be productive at their work. Which is a necessity for employees to be engaged.

Catherine, briefly describe "flow" and why it's important.

[Flavin] Flow is a mental state of being so fully engaged in a task that you lose track of time and place. In flow, you are deeply engaged, cognitively and emotionally. You experience new levels of motivation, creativity, innovation, and performance, and it is a tremendously happy, peaceful state. It's described as peak experience and peak performance—highly productive and innately worthwhile.

Is flow a state of mind or the result of an optimum environment? Are those the prerequisites to achieving flow?

[Flavin] While mindset and place matter, they are not enough. To enter flow, a person needs these three essentials:

1. A goal that you are passionate about.
2. A task on which you get clear, immediate, non-threatening feedback as you go.
3. A just-right level of real challenge—that is, enough to push you, but not so challenging that it intimidates you or makes you too anxious.

Let me give you an example. For me, analyzing data so a client can understand what their leaders or employees are saying is meaningful and challenging, but not too challenging as I have lots of training and experience at it. So was making my parent's 50th-anniversary video, pulling together decades of pictures to tell their story. At 1 a.m., my husband would have to pull me from the computer. In each case, there was something really hard and worthwhile about the task, each had a clear end game, each was challenging, and I knew how I was doing as I worked, which kept me at it as time and worries faded.

Can anyone achieve flow?

[Flavin] Yes, we all can. We may not achieve flow in the same ways. I just described some of the common elements. And for each of us, there are individualized elements too.

For starters, what you find intrinsically motivating is likely different from what I do. And we may find flow in different ways. Some of us find it in connecting with other people. Some people find it in solitude where they can deeply consider issues or information. Others find their flow in physical movement or in creating. Cultivating flow requires those common conditions and attending to those individualized factors as well.

How does an organization support flow?

[Flavin] This is a really interesting question. Organizations whose leaders do these three "basics"—big goals, real-time feedback, and the right level of challenge—really very well and consistently will foster more flow, and see the results in performance and engagement. I underscore consistency because we still see a surprising amount of variation in organizations in how effectively leaders do those things.

Beyond those basics, cultivating flow means personalizing the connection between the manager and the employee. It means bringing emotional intelligence to the next level, recognizing how each person is unique. We teach leaders to observe and "follow the employee"—that is, to watch for signs of people being intrinsically motivated by something, and to get to know skills and character strengths so those can be the grounding from which an employee stretches to meet a challenge. Those skills are essential because engagement and flow are deeply personal, emotional phenomenon.

Lastly, cultures that encourage people to block time are smart. There's a lot in normal business that works against our ability to achieve flow, such as hyper-busyness, a constant intrusion of emails, back-to-back meetings, face time pressures, etc. Our ability to focus is a valuable commodity that needs to be honored, too.

Giving Managers a Workable Office Environment

Often new managers inherit the office space of their predecessor. I get it; it's the space that was available. But if that space is not properly equipped for the person, a new manager could be left struggling to be productive. This isn't about how the office looks. It's about how the office functions.

Rebecca Greier Horton from the human factors and ergonomics division at Herman Miller (HMI), shared some suggestions in an interview with the author for giving new managers a productive new office space:

- The traditional office may not physically make sense for the new occupant. Small tweaks can be made by adding height adjustability and customizing monitor placement to maximize sightlines, making the manager's office both ergonomically agile and socially inviting.
- Ergonomic task seating is not an accessory. It's a necessity. Customized ergonomic task seating is both good for the body and can make a colorful statement reflecting the new manager's style. (Pink is my personal favorite; however, one of my former employers would not allow that choice when I was promoted!) Ergonomic task seating is used by the average office worker more than his car and, unfortunately, sometimes more than his mattress. Basic task seating should provide sacral support, thermal comfort, and minimize pressure points on the body of the user.
- New managers who are empowered to make bigger changes may consider doing away with the corner office altogether, which traditionally hogs the corner windows and views, and opt for a "living office" environment that places leaders in the midst of team members and frees the coveted corner views for a shared collaborative area. This is a powerful social and cognitive ergonomic statement but what manager wouldn't like to claim an immediate increase in morale, trust, and productivity in her department?

Horton added that HMI has measured time spent at the office with both large and small companies and observed that travel and expectation of constant connectivity keep leaders away from their office over half of the time. This could be one more reason to evolve and say goodbye to the corner office.

Ultimately, office workspaces need to allow for both collaboration and privacy. Give managers choices on how their office should be configured for maximum productivity.

At this point, you might be noticing a theme when it comes to well-being. It's about goals, feedback, communication, and change. All things we ask new managers to do exceptionally well. And I'll admit, maybe these topics are covered in other training opportunities currently being offered at your organization. But new managers need to learn these topics in the context of setting the right example for employees and coaching employees to do the same.

One company that understands the idea of promoting employee we-being is Virgin Pulse, part of Sir Richard Branson's Virgin Group, which designs technology that cultivates good lifestyle habits for employees. I spoke with January Stewart, HR manager at Virgin Pulse, about how the company infuses well-being in its onboarding programs:

> At Virgin Pulse, we help other companies improve their employee well-being. In order to do that effectively, we have to walk the talk. Starting with the first interview, we stress the importance of employee well-being and promote the wide variety of resources we offer to our team.
>
> On an employee's first day, they receive their free Max wearable device and a login to the Virgin Pulse online well-being platform. Through this program, employees are able to access educational information, triggers, and tracking tools that help them maintain their holistic well-being—from physical activity and nutrition to sleep and stress management. Employees are briefed on how they can earn cash bonuses and discounts on their health insurance premium through their participation in the program.
>
> On day one, employees also get a tour of our office space with a focus on visiting the two in-building gyms, two kitchens with free, healthy snacks, and the treadmill desks. But beyond our formal program and in-office well-being offerings, new employees are encouraged and supported in prioritizing their well-being—including taking breaks during the day to exercise or meditate. Our culture is one of the top ways we support employees because we live and breathe well-being every day.

One of the basic tenets we ask new managers to do is set the example. This doesn't apply only to technical skills and people skills.

Managers need to allow employees to bring the whole person to work. They will never be able to ask employees to give 110 percent to the team if employees are only allowed to bring their work selves into the building. To accomplish this, managers also need to bring their whole selves to work.

We have one last aspect of content to address, and I left it last intentionally because it deals with human resources. I don't want "legal stuff" to overshadow the other skills that managers must have, but it's important to address the legal obligation managers have to the organization.

Chapter 15.

Human Resource Skills

Most, if not all, of the technical, people, and well-being skills we've spoken about so far are also skills that are required of human resources. We need to have process improvement skills, communication skills, and goal-setting skills. I'm calling this chapter human resource skills because it focuses on an area the profession is well known for—employment law. But just as human resources is about more than employment law, managers need to have more HR skills than simply those related to employment law.

One of the most important aspects to HR professionals is their knowledge of labor and employment law. Organizations rely on HR to educate management about laws that apply to the workplace, investigate issues that arise, and work with legal counsel to resolve legal matters. But the only way that HR can effectively deal with an issue is if it knows about it. Yes, employees do come directly to HR to express their concerns. But the organization also needs managers to understand enough about labor law so they don't create issues. And managers have to be knowledgeable enough to bring concerns to HR when needed.

As an HR professional, I do not shy away from my employment law responsibilities. It's a part of the job. But I do feel that we don't have to bear the total weight of understanding employment law. Resources are available to help our organizations and us. One of those resources is labor lawyers.

To give some perspective on why new managers should receive some employment law training, I asked Jonathan Segal, a partner with the firm of Duane Morris LLP to share his knowledge. I've known Jonathan for years, and he has helped answer reader questions on HR Bartender for quite some time. Keep in mind that answering legal-related questions on my blog or sharing his comments in this book is not his full-time job, and his comments should not be construed as legal advice or as pertaining to any factual situations. If you have detailed questions, address them directly with your friendly neighborhood labor attorney.

Supervisory Training by Jonathan Segal

For lawyers, keeping up with the employment laws is not easy. There are federal, state, and local laws. And, then there are agency enforcement positions that, in some cases, seek to stretch the law beyond the obvious.

It is even harder for HR professionals. Yes, every good HR professional has a general understanding of most employment laws and a more in-depth understandings of others. HR training includes the law. But human resources is about so much more than just the law. We can't let lawyers take the *human* out of human resources.

Now, come our managers. Often they are promoted because they are the best at what they do. Or, they are selected because of their people skills. In almost all cases a "working knowledge of the law" is not a requirement.

Yet, most claims against companies are based on what managers do—or don't do. And, when it comes to the law, it is dangerous to assume that managers will just intuit correctly.

For example, it is human for a manager to ask an employee who seems depressed if he is. But that humanity results in a perceived disability claim under the ADA [Americans with Disabilities Act] if adverse action is taken against the employee.

Management training should provide operational guidelines within the legal framework of what managers can do, cannot do, and what they should report to HR. The training should cover from hello to goodbye with key aspects of the employment cycle in between. Here are three reasons to consider providing training to your management team:

- Minimizes the likelihood that managers will make good-faith mistakes that may result in claims.

> • Reinforces the affirmative responsibilities of managers so they know that not doing anything if they see or otherwise hear of wrongdoing may be an admission of liability and not a defense.
> • May serve as a partial defense in some claims and help minimize damages in others, depending on the nature of the claim.

In addition to new tasks, new managers face legal responsibilities. As much as we in HR want new managers to consult us on every possible incident, though, the reality is that there's just not enough HR time to go around. Managers need to understand compliance to reduce organizational risk of litigation and bad publicity. Compliance also improves recruitment process, fosters engagement, and improves retention. This positions managers to bring HR into the loop at appropriate times, so HR and managers can work with legal counsel to address issues as they relate to employees.

14 Employment Laws Every Manager Should Know

Hopefully by now you're convinced that you need to conduct employment law training for new managers. Then the question becomes . . . which employment laws? There are so many!

Table 15.1 is a list of the most common employment laws that may be worth sharing with new managers. By no means is this an exhaustive list. It is a place to start. The following list is of U.S. federal labor laws. Many states, like California,[1] have passed their own legislation, which could affect how the federal law is administered within your organization. If your organization has a global reach, country-specific laws need to be considered.

The point being, this list was created to start your thought process. I've included the name of the law, a couple of sentences explaining its scope, and a website for reference. As you're thinking about putting together an employment law session for new managers, I'd suggest consulting your friendly employment law attorney. Laws change on a regular basis, and you will want to make sure you're giving managers the most current information.

Table 15.1. The Key U.S. Employment Laws

Federal Law	Brief Description	Where to Find Information
Title VII of the Civil Rights Act	A federal law that prohibits employers from discriminating against employees on the basis of sex, race, color, national origin, or religion. It applies to employers with 15 or more employees, including federal, state, and local governments. This is also the law that prohibits sexual harassment.	http://www.eeoc.gov/laws/statutes/titlevii.cfm.
Fair Labor Standards Act	The Fair Labor Standards Act (FLSA) covers the proper compensation of employees, and includes the federal minimum wage law. It also requires employers to pay time-and-a-half overtime pay for hourly workers who work more than 40 hours per week. Also, the FLSA covers youth labor, breaks/rest periods, and travel pay. It covers the private sector as well as federal, state, and local governments	http://www.dol.gov/whd/flsa
Family and Medical Leave Act	The Family and Medical Leave Act (FMLA) says eligible employees can take up to 12 weeks per year of unpaid, job-protected leave for specified family and medical reasons with continuation of group health insurance coverage under the same terms and conditions as if the employee had not taken leave. The law applies to organizations with 50 or more employees.	http://www.dol.gov/whd/fmla
Age Discrimination in Employment Act	The Age Discrimination in Employment Act (ADEA) is the federal law covering age discrimination. The law prohibits employers from refusing to hire, terminating, or taking other discriminatory action against an employee age 40 or older, based solely on the employee's age.	http://www.eeoc.gov/laws/statutes/adea.cfm
Americans with Disabilities Act	The Americans with Disabilities Act (ADA) is a civil rights law that prohibits discrimination and ensures equal opportunity for persons with disabilities in employment, state, and local government services, public accommodations, commercial facilities, and transportation.	http://www.ada.gov
Uniformed Services Employment and Reemployment Rights Act	The Uniformed Services Employment and Reemployment Rights Act (USERRA) is a federal law that establishes rights and responsibilities for uniformed service members and their civilian employers.	http://www.dol.gov/vets/programs/userra

continued on next page

Table 15.1. The Key U.S. Employment Laws (continued)

Federal Law	Brief Description	Where to Find Information
Equal Pay Act	The Equal Pay Act (EPA) is a federal law amending the FLSA, aimed at abolishing wage disparities based on sex. It requires that men and women in the same workplace be given equal pay for equal work.	http://www.eeoc.gov/laws/statutes/epa.cfm
Employee Retirement Income Security Act	The Employee Retirement Income Security Act (ERISA) a federal law that sets minimum standards for most voluntarily established pension and health plans in private industry to provide protection for the individuals in these plans.	http://www.dol.gov/general/topic/health-plans/erisa
Occupational Safety and Health Act	The Occupational Safety and Health Act (OSH Act) was created to reduce workplace hazards and implement safety and health programs for both employers and their employees.	https://www.osha.gov
Pregnancy Discrimination Act	The Pregnancy Discrimination Act (PDA) is an amendment to Title VII of the Civil Rights Act prohibits discrimination on the basis of pregnancy, childbirth, or related medical conditions.	http://www.eeoc.gov/laws/statutes/pregnancy.cfm
Immigration Reform and Control Act	The Immigration Reform and Control Act (IRCA) is a federal law passed to control and deter illegal immigration to the United States. Its provisions include criminalization of knowingly hiring an individual who is not eligible to work in the United States. It also introduced the Form I-9 to ensure employees present proper proof of work eligibility.	http://www.uscis.gov
National Labor Relations Act	The National Labor Relations Act (NLRA) protects the rights of employees and employers, encourages collective bargaining, and curtails private-sector labor and management practices that can harm workers. It applies to both union and nonunion work environments.	https://www.nlrb.gov/resources/national-labor-relations-act
Section 1981 of the Civil Rights Act of 1866	This law protects the equal right of all persons to make and enforce contracts without respect to race. This includes all contractual aspects of the employment relationship, such as hiring, discharge, and the terms and conditions of employment.	http://www.eeoc.gov/laws/other.cfm#cra-1866
Genetic Information Nondiscrimination Act	The Genetic Information Nondiscrimination Act (GINA) is a federal law that protects individuals from genetic discrimination in health insurance and employment. Genetic discrimination is defined as the misuse of genetic information.	http://www.eeoc.gov/laws/types/genetic.cfm

As you're thinking about the different pieces of legislation that new managers need to know, it's possible that employment law isn't the only type. Certain industries or professions might have laws that govern their activities as well. When I worked in the transportation industry, we were subject to different laws, even from an employment perspective.

In your manager onboarding program, this information can be presented in several different formats. You could offer an employment law workshop for new managers with refresher sessions as laws change for current managers.[2] The workshop could be held in a classroom or videotaped and distributed to participants.

I've worked at companies that brought their (in-house or outside) legal counsel in for a manager lunch and presentation. The managers responded well to the lunch-and-learn concept. The method used to present this information could change based on your staffing analysis. In years when you anticipate a lot of legislative activity, the information could be conveyed via video or podcast, and in years when you expect less legislative activity, the information could be included with new-manager orientation. I see this as one of those areas where organizations have flexibility. What I don't see is organizations ignoring it completely. Managers need to understand their responsibilities.

Building Mutually Beneficial Working Relationships between Managers and HR

Speaking of responsibilities, an additional benefit to including an employment law component in manager onboarding is the opportunity to start building relationships with new managers. Human resources needs to work with new managers on recruitment, employee relations, training and development, performance management, and other topics. The relationship that managers have with HR is based on trust and mutual respect.

This is an opportunity to educate new managers on the role of human resources and on how a strategic business partnership is formed. HR professionals will always be the go-to department for employment law matters. We can't be territorial and not share some foundational information with managers. Our jobs will not be in jeopardy if managers know employment law basics. In fact, quite the opposite.

Managers having an understanding of employment law will allow human resources to focus on some of the more transformational and strategic initiatives taking place in the organization and to find time to work on big-picture issues like succession planning and management development—both directly related to manager onboarding. Reducing the amount of time spent on legal compliance could be a good thing for everyone involved.

I think one of the best ways to demonstrate how sharing HR knowledge benefits the entire organization is to look at an organization that provides HR services. This is an organization that needs to set the example.

iCIMS is the leading provider of software-as-a-service (SaaS) talent acquisition solutions. Based in New Jersey, it is a privately held and profitable organization with over 3,000 contracted customers and 4,500 clients worldwide. I had the chance to speak with Susan Vitale, the company's chief marketing officer, about the company's onboarding process.

iCIMS has a comprehensive onboarding program that provides new hires with a strong foundation on the corporate culture, mission, vision, values, solutions, and customer service commitment. The first week of onboarding includes sessions on everything from corporate strategies to process overviews, as well as an overview of the iCIMS Talent Acquisition Software Suite and face-to-face meetings with key teams throughout the organization.

From offering assistance in tasks like creating an e-mail signature to introducing new hires to the company's entire executive team, its onboarding program encompasses everything employees need to get acquainted with iCIMS, the company culture, and their new colleagues. Currently, the firm's offerings are classroom-based, and it is working toward adding some of the curriculum to its learning management system (LMS). The bulk of classroom training lasts about four days, after which domain-specific onboarding occurs at the department level.

Vitale shared that iCIMS' onboarding program is a collaborative effort between marketing and HR:

Our marketing team partnered closely with human resources to create the content that is shared and the result is sessions that are informative yet fun, visually appealing, and engaging. In fact, following the roll out of our new onboarding materials, we have experienced an uptick in employee referrals from new hires that we are in part attributing to the success of this marketing and HR collaboration. The program includes a scavenger hunt that encourages new hires to explore the buildings within our headquarters.

iCIMS conducts a Managing at iCIMS program approximately five or six times per year, depending on the need, that involves every newly hired people manager at iCIMS. Typically offered within the managers' first few weeks at the company, the two-day program allows newer management hires to network with one another and receive detailed training on its management processes and systems. I really like that the curriculum also provides incredible opportunities to sit down with a panel of managers who recently went through the program, as well as with the CEO and chief financial officer (CFO), who reveal tips and strategies that will enable the managers to lead their teams successfully at iCIMS.

Vitale also shared the team's noteworthy discovery while designing the program:

Before the latest redesign of our onboarding process, we were providing new hires with too much information that they were not ready or able to process during their first week of employment. We had to take a hard look at our existing materials and prune them down considerably to improve the impact the communications had on new hires and ensure that our mission, vision, values and executional framework were effectively shared with everyone—regardless of their placement within the organization. It took some time to analyze all of the information and decide which points we would focus on. Our goal was to provide the most important information to accelerate assimilation. That said, since we are a rapidly growing company, we need to continuously evolve our onboarding process to make sure it meets the needs of our business as we scale.

In this section, we've covered a lot of skills that managers need to know. The goal isn't to give managers all of these skills immediately upon hire or promotion. As Vitale shared, the goal is to identify what managers need to know and when they need to know it. Which brings us to our next section on post-onboarding activities.

After new managers have been welcomed into the organization or their new department, and . . .

After they've attended some sort of new-manager orientation, and . . .

After they've maybe had a few one-on-ones with their boss, . . .

The chances are that the new managers are on their own, *but* they're not done with the learning process.

In the next section, we'll talk about some of the programs that organizations can create to support their post-onboarding efforts.

Part V:

Post-Onboarding Strategies

"The beautiful thing about learning is nobody can take it away from you."

—B.B. King

Chapter 16.

Career Development

Once the formal onboarding process is completed, managers still need to learn a lot of information. You can't cover everything in onboarding. And the changing pace of business demands that employees have a plan for future learning and development.

Although I agree that employees need to own their careers, on some level, I think organizations need to acknowledge that we haven't done much to teach employees how to do that. Managers need to know how they like to learn, how to find relevant resources, and how to apply learning to their work.

If we want managers to be in control of their careers, we need to give them the tools to do it effectively. That's part of teaching them to be successful. Set expectations for what they will be responsible for developing and what the organization will help them with. If we do that well, then they will be able to do the same for their employees.

Career Management versus Career Development

I draw a distinction between career management and career development, so I want to take a moment to explain them both. Career management is focused on what the organization wants in the employee's career. Career development is what the employee wants in *his or her* career. Ideally, we want these two concepts to align: What the employee wants from his or her career is the same as the company, and they work together to achieve the same goal.

Unfortunately, that doesn't always happen. This doesn't mean the company is bad or wrong. Or that the employee isn't a team player. It means the company's goals and the employee's goals aren't in alignment. Something needs to happen. And what that "something" is really depends on the individuals involved. But I will say this—it doesn't have to be an ugly situation.

I've mentioned earlier in the book that I used to work in the hospitality industry. At one point in my career, my boss took me out to lunch and told me that he thought I would be a good general manager. I was incredibly flattered. He told me the skills and attributes that I already possessed would make me a good general manager. And he told me the things that I would have to learn. One of the things that I'd need to do is leave human resources and work in other departments.

Well, I really had to think about it. Becoming a general manager was not something that I originally had in my plans. The prospect was intriguing, but I liked human resources. Ultimately, I went back to my boss and told him where my heart was. But I also thought he brought up some valid points about things I needed to learn. I thought those topics would make me a better HR professional. So while I stayed in HR, I did gain exposure to aspects of the operation I don't know that I would have otherwise.

The point of my story is this—in our careers, we will be presented with new opportunities. We need to evaluate them and make wise career decisions. This isn't a skill we teach people in school. Giving managers some insight into career management and career development will benefit not only them but the rest of the organization.

How to Make Good Career Decisions

The reason we need to teach managers how to make good career decisions is because organizations could be setting themselves up for a big surprise if they make the assumption that everyone wants to move up within the company. It's simply not always true. Yes, some employees will, but others might not want the opportunity. This is another reason (see Chapter 6) that telling employees that they are part of the succession plan makes sense.

No matter what career path you are pursuing, you should be able to answer a few specific questions about your career:

Think of the moment in your life when you were feeling most productive, most healthy, most successful, most self-fulfilled. What was happening in your life at that time? What was the situation that made you feel that way? Describe in some detail the specifics of the situation, how you felt in that situation, how you felt about yourself, and how you behaved.

Ultimately, every career decision a person makes should align with the answers to these questions. Whether that's accepting a promotion, taking a transfer, changing companies, whatever . . . that career decision should help each of us feel productive, healthy, and successful. If it doesn't, then we should ask ourselves, "Why am I doing this?"

Figuring out the answer to these questions takes time, self-awareness, and serious thought. The answer won't arrive in a flash. It might evolve over time. The point is each of us needs to figure out what our most productive state looks like and then make career decisions that will take us there.

Also, it's possible that a career decision will move you closer to your most productive state without completely getting there. And that could be valuable. It's about recognizing what your career decision will do for you.

In my experience, I've found when employees talked to me about not being happy and satisfied in their careers, they were making career decisions that moved them away from being their most productive, healthy, and self-fulfilled. They made decisions contrary to the answers above and focused on getting *away* from something.

Once we know our most productive state, we need to start practicing how to articulate it: "I'm at my most productive when I'm doing [insert most productive activity]." People should look for activities in their current roles that they can use as an example. For instance, "I'm my most productive when I'm able to be enterprising. For example, when I was able to volunteer for the health and wellness fair committee without asking permission first."

Once employees feel they can comfortably articulate their most productive state, they should do three things to help their career opportunities:

1. *Share this information with their manager.* They should include this information in conversations with their manager during one-on-one meetings and performance reviews. Employees' managers cannot help them become their most productive when they don't know what it takes. This information helps managers understand the employees and the types of career opportunities they want in the future.

2. *Respond to opportunities in the context of their productive state.* If employees are presented with a career opportunity that doesn't excite them, they should decline the offer using their productivity as a reason. They can say, "That sounds like a great opportunity. I've found that I'm at my least productive when I'm doing [insert least productive activity]. So I don't know that I'm a good fit for this assignment."

3. *Assert your productive state during meetings.* Every once in a while, we attend a meeting at which we know we're going to leave with an assignment. Instead of trying to avoid the inevitable and ending up with a work assignment you don't like, volunteer early for an assignment that aligns with your most productive state. If you have to take on more work, why not take on work that you will enjoy?

I wish I could say these strategies work every time, but we all know there are times when we will have to do work that doesn't align with our most productive state. The goal isn't to eliminate all forms of least productive work. It's to spend the vast majority of our time doing our most productive work. That's when we know we're making good career decisions.

What Employees Should Do During Each Stage of Their Career

I mentioned earlier that our career goals evolve over time. In fact, they will change depending on where we are in our careers. Our goals at the beginning of our careers probably aren't the same as they are later in our careers. Managers need guidance for themselves and their employees as they transition through the different stages of their careers.

Early Career: Establishing Your Long-Term Goals

The early-career phase can take on two different looks. First, it can be the time when employees have their first few jobs and are learning those skills that make them great employees. Examples might be working with occupational schedules, dress codes, and company policies and procedures. It can also be their first job in what they consider their chosen profession. During the early-career phase, employees should:

- Discuss with management the traditional career path for the profession. It's difficult to set career goals without knowing all the options.
- Find out the skills and experience needed for future promotional opportunities. And discover how to go about acquiring those skills.
- Be prepared to share long-term career goals and commitment to achieving those goals. Don't make the assumption that the organization automatically knows the plan.

Midcareer: Dedication to Your Profession

During the midcareer phase, employees are considered generalists or specialists in their chosen fields. They manage programs, processes, or people. And they can hold a formal title within the organization, such as manager or director. In this phase, employees want to consider these activities:

- Reevaluate and confirm career goals. Sometimes the goals employees have early in their careers are not the goals they have later in their careers.
- Talk with management about multidirectional career paths. Employees can gain valuable experience by considering a lateral move or even a downgrade (no, it's not *always* a bad thing) to a different department.
- Find out about certifications and credentials to support their profession. Establishing mastery of professional knowledge can elevate an employee's career.

Late Career: Sharing Your Knowledge and Expertise

In the late-career phase, employees are considered highly experienced in their roles. Employees in this stage might be formally or informally considering semiretirement or some planned exit strategy. Employees in the late-career stage will want to:

- Discuss with management about participating in company mentoring programs. Knowledge management is a huge issue, and employees have an opportunity to share their extensive knowledge.
- Reevaluate learning opportunities. Employees today realize they need to be constantly learning, even during the latter part of a career.
- Explore new job assignments and role adjustments. If a second act—a major role adjustment—is part of the career plan, what do those roles and responsibilities look like?

This is probably a good time to mention that career stages aren't driven by age. Newly promoted managers may go from a late-career stage as an employee to an early-career stage as a new manager. Or a midcareer manager may transfer to a new division and thus move to an early-career stage. Many people have multiple careers in their lifetime, so they go through the phases more than once.

Regardless of the career stage, employees need to dedicate time to discovering what they would like to pursue. They need to articulate their career goals to the company so that management can support them. Speaking of which, the organization needs to do its part in helping employees have successful careers.

What Organizations Should Do During Each Stage of an Employee's Career

Employees have a role in the process of career management and steps that they are individually responsible for. Even though I've suggested that companies need to help employees learn these strategies, the employee is still ultimately responsible for making them happen.

Career management isn't a one-sided activity. Organizations are an equal partner in the process. Employees regularly make decisions about their careers based on the perceived support (or nonsupport) from the company, which affects employee engagement and retention.

Managers need to know how to have career conversations with employees. These discussions aren't formulaic and don't follow a checklist. They are as unique as the employee and the stage of an employee's career.

Early Career: Understanding Employee Goals and Aspirations

During this phase, employees are trying to determine their future. They might be choosing a profession or evaluating which path within their profession bests suits them. They could also be wondering how the organization fits into those long-term plans. During the early-career phase, the company should:

- Make sure employees know the career path that is available—within their current role, the department, and the organization.
- Share with employees tools and resources that can help them determine their career goals. This could be in the form of workshops, books, videos, online tools, assessments, etc.
- Commit to supporting the employee's goals. The process of defining a career path takes time and can often change. Don't try to read an employee's mind where his or her career goals are concerned.

Midcareer: Supporting Growth and Learning Opportunities

In midcareer, employees are looking to refine their knowledge and skills. It's possible they will explore opportunities outside of their department or the organization. Managers need to trust that employees will make the right decisions about their careers and play the role of coach. Companies should consider these activities:

- Find opportunities for employees to develop skills while staying in their current role. Assignments on task forces or project teams can be valuable for the employee and the company.
- Listen and consider employee proposals to redesign work responsibilities. As the business world changes, so do careers. Let employees have a voice in job design.

- Encourage education and learning. Whether it's in-house training or outside learning programs, suggest and recommend opportunities for employees to expand their knowledge.

Late Career: Demonstrating Respect and Encouraging Sharing

Employees in the late-career stage have a history with the company. They hold a significant amount of knowledge that the organization needs. It's possible they have a clearly designed plan for the future. It's also possible that they are looking for the company to be flexible with their needs. During this stage, companies need to:

- Consider alternative career strategies such as contingent work to retain highly knowledgeable and valuable workers.
- Encourage employees to share their expertise with new employees as part of a buddy system. Or design a mentoring program in which employees can share expertise.
- Respect employee career decisions. It might not be the decision the organization was hoping for, but it's possible that the employee might reconsider at a later time.

The career decisions an employee makes have a tremendous impact on the organization. It's in a company's best interest to support, encourage, nurture, and respect employees' careers. The people who will do that for the company are managers. The support and investment a manager makes in an employee's future creates employee engagement, increases productivity, and improves the bottom line.

How to Sell Management on Attending a Conference

In the last section, I mentioned giving employees resources to help them with their career goals. A major resource in professional development is professional conferences. Just because you're creating a manager onboarding program doesn't mean that you're eliminating the need for professional development.

But going to conferences can be difficult—specifically, the part where you're trying to sell senior management on spending the money for attendance. I have been in this position many times. Even now, as a consultant, I still use the lessons I learned from pitching conferences to my manager when I have to make decisions regarding attending conferences. There are dozens of events out there, and unless your job requires you to attend conferences, you have to figure out the best ones to commit your resources.

We need to teach managers how to pitch their professional development, not only for themselves but also so they know how to evaluate employee requests for professional development. Here's how to research an event.

Find the best conferences for you. It's tempting to attend an event because it's in a fun location or because all the cool kids are going to be there. If money is no object, then by all means go. Conferences need to produce a return on your investment. So think about what you want to learn and then start searching for the right events to supply it.

Ask the right questions. Reaching out to respected colleagues about conferences to attend could be a good idea. The important part is asking the right question, "What were your takeaways from the event?" If you get a blank stare, that doesn't necessarily mean the conference isn't worth your time. But do try to find out the value of attendance from a colleague's perspective.

Learning takes place in many ways. Speaking of learning, it's vital to understand how you like to learn (that is, visual, auditory, kinesthetic). For instance, there are certain topics that I want to learn by reading a book. I would not attend a conference for those topics. But for others, I want to learn differently, and a conference is a perfect format.

Learning happens in many places. Yes, learning happens during educational sessions. Don't forget that learning also takes place during networking and on the expo hall floor. And occasionally at the bar or in a coffee shop with colleagues.

So you have completed the research and identified an event. Now what? Before discussing the conference with a manager, be prepared to answer some questions. These are the types of questions that my manager used to ask me:

1. *Conference:* What organization hosts this conference? How long has it been around? How often does it have conferences? Does it offer regional events? Are you a member?

2. *Cost:* How much will attending this event cost? How much is registration versus travel? Are you prepared to share in the cost of the trip?
3. *Takeaways:* What do you expect to learn? Is there another way to learn this information? How will it affect your job today? And how will it affect the company?
4. *Work:* How will your work be handled while you are gone?
5. *Follow-up:* What is your plan for sharing information when you return?

These might seem like a lot of questions. But I can't tell you how many times I've seen an employee bring a conference brochure to a manager without thinking about the cost, his or her work, or the follow-up. If the manager doesn't ask, that's fine, but at least you will be prepared.

Going to a conference can be a great way to learn. But if we're going to create a culture in which employees own their career development, then we need to teach them how to do the homework. And it's possible that, in doing the homework, employees will discover whether this is the right event for them.

Choosing the Right Assessment Tools for Your Organization

While conferences and professional development events certainly add value to an employee's career, internal activities can bring equal value. I mentioned that career management isn't a one-sided activity. And it's not. We've talked about the conversations managers and employees need to have about the employee's career. For a second, let's talk about the conversations employees and managers need to have about the manager's career.

Yes, that's right. We need to teach managers how to accept feedback from their employees and how to process that feedback and use it for their own career development. This conversation about careers is not a downward-flowing dialogue. At least, it doesn't have to be.

One way to facilitate upward career development conversations is by using assessments. I once had a boss who, every time he took an assessment, would share a copy of it with his direct reports. At first I thought this was just weird. But then I realized he was doing me a favor because he was telling me how to manage him. Many new managers don't realize how important it is to tell employees how to manage up. So assessments could be a way for new managers to get comfortable with themselves and with sharing information about themselves with employees.

There are many assessments on the market. Any organization considering an assessment should research the available options. Years ago, I spoke with Julie Moreland, senior vice president at PeopleClues, a global provider of employment assessments for measuring job fit, attitude, and level of engagement for candidates and employees. If you're new to working with assessments (whether it's for hiring or development), you'll find Julie's comments helpful.

For starters, how would you define an assessment? Do you consider it to be the same as a profile, survey, or test?

[Moreland] It's an interesting question, some of these terms are interchangeable [and semantics] but there are some differences:

- A survey captures data with no right or wrong answer intended, more the ability to compare and look for trends in the information. An example would be an employee satisfaction survey.
- A test implies that there are right or wrong answers, and this term is often used with testing for skills or knowledge such as the ability level to use Microsoft Excel or Word.
- In our industry, an assessment generally refers to something that measures an individual on a set of criteria and compares their answers against benchmarked data to be used for screening, selection, development, and leadership identification. They aim to help the employer learn more about an individual's preferences and core behaviors that impact job fit and job satisfaction.

Let's say my company has never used an assessment before. Tell me what an assessment can do for my business. I'm not necessarily talking about a specific assessment but just in general.

[Moreland] Valid and predictive assessments will help organizations calibrate their screening and selection processes with objective data, and give a greater understanding of the factors that make an individual successful at their company and in specific roles. It becomes your people-business-intelligence data that becomes an objective data-point for workforce planning. A highly effective assessment implementation will also be user friendly and stream-line the processes internally. The three critical benefits of using assessments are:

1. Bring objective information in the hiring process to make it more legally defensible and efficient (don't spend precious HR time with applicants who don't have a basic fit for the position).

2. Create a more focused and efficient interview by using behavioral questions from the assessment results to have a quicker and more focused interview. Assessments help avoid the pitfalls of managers who haven't been trained in interviewing but are responsible for knowing what they should and shouldn't ask (they have a specific process and questions to follow to create more consistency).

3. Pre-employment assessments can help employers gain better insight to their candidates to improve quality of hire and reduce turnover. By better understanding the individuals' skills, behaviors and preferences, companies are equipped to make better hiring decisions. Assessment reports can also be used to develop employees and teams and identify and groom potential leaders.

Is there anything an assessment can't do?

[Moreland] In order for an assessment to be successful and legal, it cannot and should not be the only data point in the people process for a company. Assessments are designed to measure specific characteristics with people, some measure more broadly and some more specific. So, there will always [be] something a hiring manager may want to know that the given assessment can't measure, because it's designed to measure something else.

What advice would you give to a company when deciding which assessment to choose?

[Moreland] When evaluating assessments for your pre-employment selection and workforce development processes, there are a number of factors that you should consider:

1. Is the assessment right for the situation? Some assessments are geared more toward management and are long and expensive. Others are geared more toward your general population of applicants and are quick and inexpensive. You may need both, but often companies use good assessments but not as efficiently and cost-effectively as they could be.

2. Is the assessment easily interpretable? Make sure you're picking assessments that don't require your hiring managers to become experts in interpretation! The assessment ideally will be benchmarked and create a job fit profile that matches your jobs, so that the reporting is job relevant and doesn't need interpretation.

3. Is it valid and reliable? Ask the assessment provider for the technical manuals that illustrate how valid, legally defensible and predictive their assessment is. You'll need this information to be confident that your processes are compliant and reliable.

4. Is it easily accessible via your technology? How technically capable is the assessment company? In an ideal world, the assessment should quickly integrate into your HR technology for ease of use and a seamless recruiter/hiring manager and candidate experience.

One of the downfalls I've seen with assessments is when companies become too reliant on a single instrument and use it for the wrong purposes. What would you say to a company that is looking for a one-size-fits-all approach to assessments?

[Moreland] Assessments are not and cannot be a silver bullet; they are designed to provide additional insight and inform decisions, not make them. There are at least three areas that should be explored with applicants. Job fit for sure, but also attitudes and skills, which can be explored within interviews and resumes.

By relying solely on assessment results, employers risk missing out on other key information to determine which applicants are the best fit overall for their organization. This is the opposite of the intended purpose and outcomes when including assessments in talent acquisition and management practices. It is possible to choose an assessment that can work across your entire organization, but benchmarking is critical to make sure you're measuring your jobs, so that the reporting is job relevant.

Another challenge I've witnessed is when companies are afraid to start using or stop using an assessment out of fear of being sued. Can you offer one or two things companies need to consider when they have to make changes involving assessments?

[Moreland] A good best practice is to consult their legal counsel. In doing so, they'll likely learn that consistency and documentation are key to compliant assessment practices.

Another important step is to conduct a benchmarking study and overall analysis of their hiring process to see if the assessment they are currently using or thinking of using is actually job relevant and isn't creating disparate impact.

Are you seeing any trends in assessments that business professionals should start paying attention to?

[Moreland] It is widely accepted by the psychological world that we can reliably and predictably measure cognitive ability and behavioral traits ("The Big Five" of Conscientiousness, Extraversion, Stability, Tough-Mindedness, and Conventionality), so once you go outside of these measures, you may be using an assessment that is not widely accepted or documented.

Assessments that aim to measure "social" and "cultural" fit—which are currently hot topics for recruiting—are garnering a lot of interest recently, but these are qualities that are complicated and difficult to determine through a single assessment measure. The industry has also seen several new assessments that don't have much science behind them, which is why employers should ask about technical manuals and validation. It's better to be safe than to learn these details about the assessment in court.

Managers Have Two Roles in Career Development

It's hard enough to manage our own careers. New managers are tasked with learning their own role and developing their employees at the same time. We need to give them tools. By teaching new managers about career development, they can successfully manage their own careers and pass along their knowledge to employees.

But career development is a topic that can be shared over time. It doesn't necessarily need to be in a formal manager onboarding workshop. It could be a special event for managers once a year or an occasional lunch-and-learn session facilitated by human resources. But it does need to be a priority, and it does need to happen. Career development should not be an afterthought.

In our next chapter, we'll talk about another form of career development that doesn't need as much structure but can yield valuable results—networking groups.

Chapter 17.

Alumni Groups and Internal Networking Groups

Many sentences in this book include the wording "managers need to know this . . . " And it's true—new managers need to know a lot of information. But the responsibility for teaching them does not have to rest 100 percent with human resources. Or with the new manager's boss.

When you create the work environment we're talking about, where managers are onboarded well, then the organization can allow communities of knowledge to form. Managers can learn from each other because the company has created management experts. Allow managers to support and encourage each other.

I view alumni and internal networking groups as being different from coaching and mentoring, which we will cover in the next chapter. These groups are informal communities in which managers can find answers to questions they may not want to ask their boss or human resources.

On a side note, I've always been a fan of collaborative hiring because it too provides additional people for new employees to learn from. In collaborative hiring, the candidate meets many people during the process. Therefore, when the new employee starts the job, he or she already knows several people in the organization. So when situations arise in which the new employee needs to understand the "unwritten rules" of the organization (and we both know they will), the employee can reach out to someone besides his or her boss and human resources. Obviously, this approach does add time to the overall hiring process, but the benefits can be worth it.

The same applies to new managers. It's one of the reasons networking is a skill that should be included with manager onboarding. New managers need a network of other managers to support them. If managers are hired from the outside, who do they know? Who can teach them the unwritten rules of the company? A few times in my career, as a manager job candidate, I've had the chance to speak with my peer group. It made a big difference when I started the job.

If the manager is being promoted from within, having supportive peers is equally important. This person is going from being "one of the gang" to being the gang's supervisor. He or she needs a support group. The tendency to think of managers as "experts" versus just competent puts extra pressure on a new manager.

In today's business world, I believe we all have a bit of subject matter expert (SME) in us. So a manager's role isn't to show everyone he or she is an expert. A challenge develops when (a) people claim to be an expert in something they know little or nothing about (for instance, I should never claim to be an expert in mowing the lawn; I don't know how to start the lawnmower) or (b) others rely on people as if they were an expert when they're not. No one should call me about cooking on the grill because, even though I'm a foodie, I'm not a grilling expert.

New managers often run into challenges because they're trying to earn the label of expert when, at this point, they should be focused on demonstrating their knowledge and competence. Oh, and let's not forget managing their team of employees who all feel *they* have a little piece of expert in them as well.

On Being an Expert

Sometimes new managers, especially those promoted from within, can be challenged by existing employees, who feel the new manager's promotion wasn't deserved. HR and the new manager's boss need to work with the new manager to help him or her become comfortable in the new role.

Often we are conditioned to think that we're being conceited or arrogant if we say we're an expert. We're only allowed to accept the "expert" label if someone else gives it to us. And then we're supposed to hem and haw about it, "Oh me?! Gosh no, I'm no expert," until someone firmly tells us to stop it. Neither approach is good when you're trying to establish your competence.

To become comfortable talking about expertise, new managers need to know what they are experts in. It's called knowing what you do well. And they should be able to articulate those things they do well along with the activities they participated in to learn the "thing" they're an expert in. Here's an example of what someone should be able to say:

> I'm an expert in designing training programs. I learned the principles of training design taking course work at ABC University. I was able to take what I learned in class and immediately apply it in a company project to revamp our existing onboarding program. My work with the onboarding program led me to be selected as the project lead to design the company's leadership development program. I'm particularly proud of this program because it was recognized by the local professional training association as one of the best leadership initiatives in the state.

New managers need to be able to comfortably discuss their achievements, especially in today's workplaces, where everyone is an SME about something.

Once the new manager is comfortable in his or her role and has been accepted by the team, it's easier for others on the team to feel confident about their level of expertise, versus thinking the new manager is the only expert. Organizations can inspire employees to embrace their successes. Employees should share their expertise with others. Having more than one expert in a subject is a great thing.

Managers just need guidance on how to manage themselves in a workforce of experts, including, possibly, managing someone who has more expertise in a subject than they do. Ultimately, it's about new managers being able to leverage the strengths of their team.

Using Social Media Platforms to Build Knowledge

While I do think it's important for managers to have an internal support system, an external support system is equally valuable. One of the best places to develop an external support system is on social media. Through social media, managers have access to a wealth of information they can learn from and share with their team. Most social platforms don't have an expense to join, making it a no-cost way for managers to network.

SHRM Connect

If you're not aware, the Society for Human Resource Management (SHRM) has an online community for HR professionals called SHRM Connect. It's a place where you can ask questions, get answers, and discuss topics relevant to the profession. For instance, it offers groups focused on functions such as HR technology and organizational development. There are also groups for the Annual Conference so individuals attending can connect with peers. Check it out when you get a chance. It might provide some creative inspiration for your manager onboarding program.

While the purpose of this section isn't to tell anyone what social media platforms to engage with or to suggest an organization's social media policy, there are three social activities that managers might want to consider are:

1. *LinkedIn groups.* LinkedIn is the world's largest professional network on the Internet with more than 400 million members in over 200 countries. Professionals sign up to join LinkedIn at the rate of approximately two per second. Over 39 million students and graduates are on LinkedIn; it's the fastest-growing demographic on the site.

   According to the blog *Undercover Recruiter*, the majority of LinkedIn users belong to groups.[1] Groups are just that—online groups where members of the group share information and articles. Groups can be focused on a profession (for example, SHRM has a LinkedIn group). They can also be focused on an activity such as SHRM Certification or an event like the HR Technology Conference. Trust me when I say there's a group for just about everything (and I don't mean that in a bad way).

2. *Facebook groups.* According to Facebook, its mission is "to give people the power to share and make the world more connected." The site has one billion daily active users, with almost 90 percent of them accessing the platform using a mobile device.

   Facebook offers groups as well, but the administrator of the group has some options when it comes to members. Groups can be visible to all Facebook users. They can also be secret, visible only to group members. For example, I've been invited to a couple of secret groups to test software. Once the testing period is over, the group disbands. While the mention of a secret group might initially be unsettling, it does come in handy for activities like testing or for a workshop, in which the group members are defined and the purpose is focused.

3. *Twitter chats.* According to Twitter, its mission is "to give everyone the power to create and share ideas and information instantly." One of the unique features of Twitter is that messages are limited to 140 characters. The platform has 320 million monthly active users, with 80 percent active on mobile devices.

   Another distinct feature of Twitter is something called a #hashtag. It's a word or phrase preceded by the pound sign (#), and it's used to identify a specific topic on Twitter. Users can search Twitter by using hashtags. Let's say you wanted to see everything that was happening at the SHRM Annual Conference: You could, for example, search in Twitter for #SHRM16, and all of the Tweets with that hashtag would show up.

   The reason Twitter is valuable is that groups of people can get together on a certain day and time to chat. For example, SHRM has a Twitter chat called #NextChat. Each week a different person leads the chat about an HR topic. Lots of Twitter chats exist, so managers are likely to find a chat that they would have an interest in.

There are many other ways to engage on social media, but these three are some of the most popular. New managers (and not-so-new managers) might enjoy the interaction with their peers. It's both interesting and exciting to see different views from a global audience.

Now, if I haven't convinced you yet that there's a good reason to have managers build an internal as well as an external network, let me toss out one more—employee referrals.[2] Yes, managers need to build networks for themselves, but they also need to build networks to help find future talent for the organization.

High-Performing Employees Refer Better Candidates

HR thought leader and professor, John Sullivan, writing for TLNT.com, referenced the study, "The Value of Hiring through [Employee] Referrals,"[3] which compared the profit impact differential between referrals from high-, average-, and low-performing employees. He concluded that high-performer referrals produce three times more impact than a below-average performer.[4] And the referral was 10 percent to 30 percent less likely to leave.

New managers who are onboarded well should perform well within the organization. They should manage their teams well, and those employees should be excellent performers. Hence, the referrals made by those managers and their teams should be excellent candidates for consideration. As the manager onboarding program becomes entrenched in the organization, the impact will be felt in more areas than just manager performance.

SilkRoad Technology, a leading provider of global cloud-based talent management solutions, reported that employee referrals are the top source of interviews (57 percent) and hires (61 percent).[5] Similar findings were shared by China Gorman, former chief operating officer for SHRM, on her blog. She cited the 2015 CareerXRoads *Source of Hire* report, which indicated that almost 30 percent of its members hired between 26 percent to 50 percent of their candidates from employee referrals.[6] Bottom line: Employee referrals are an important source of talent. But the only way to get the best referrals is by having a high-performing workforce and a culture that supports talent development.

The message here is simple—let managers build the relationships they need to be successful. They will repay you with top referrals.

Boomerang Employees

Another obvious source of talent is boomerang employees. These are individuals who used to work for the organization and come back. In some places, they might be called rehires.

Unfortunately, companies don't tap into this resource nearly enough. We think about referrals but forget about former employees. Over the years, I've worked for companies that placed a great emphasis on rehired or boomerang employees. We even dedicated time and resources to having a strategy that would encourage boomerangs. There are several reasons why:

- *The company knows them.* Boomerang employees have a history of proven skills with the organization. Their strengths are known. Their accomplishments are recorded on performance appraisals. Their personality and demeanor are remembered by co-workers and management.
- *They might have increased skills and experience.* Consider this: While those former employees haven't been working for you, they've been gaining knowledge and experience that they could never get with your organization. They bring a new perspective. That has value.
- *They know the company.* Every organization has its quirks and flaws. Guess what? Chances are former employees know them. And if they're talking with you about coming back, chances are pretty good that they can live with them.

One other thing to remember—former employees know other potential candidates (and customers!). Even if former employees are not ready or willing to discuss coming back, they can still be raving fans of your company. They can still share your job openings with friends who would be a good fit or refer potential customers to the company's product or service.

This ties back to manager networking on so many levels. A former manager might want to return to the company. A current manager might know a candidate who's interested in a managerial position with the company. When the organization is open about networking, it creates these opportunities, which is a good thing for the company's talent strategy.

Encouraging Boomerang Employees and Referrals

Former employees can be stellar future employees. Organizations need to include them in their staffing plans. Here are three strategies to consider:

1. *Treat exiting employees with respect.* I know it sounds obvious, but when employees resign, wish them well—even if you don't exactly get along, and even when employees resign at the worst possible time. Take the high road, even if they mention a few complaints in their exit interviews.

   Boomerang employees don't have to return to the same job with the same boss. They don't have to return to the same status (that is, a full-time employee might come back part time). It's possible the employee would be a perfect fit in another department. It's also possible the employee has learned how good he or she had it when working with you.

2. *Have a defined offboarding process.* Part of giving employees respect is providing a consistent offboarding process. Make sure employees receive information about COBRA, final paychecks, etc. Encourage them to participate in an exit interview. Maybe create an alumni network for former employees to receive ongoing information about the company.

   Offboarding is the last impression the employee has of the company. It's an opportunity. Do you want it to be efficient, effective, and thoughtful or inconsistent, disorganized, and incomplete?

3. *Allow former employees to stay in touch.* Just because employees no longer work for the organization doesn't mean you have to stop talking with them. I know, this sounds like another obvious remark, but I know employers that view former employees as being "against" them.

   Depending on the situation, former employees might be willing to do some freelance work for the company. It's a great way for them to stay in touch. It's also possible you will run into them during professional association or industry events. And of course, you can connect with them on social media.

New managers in the organization are also hiring managers. They need to develop a network for their own professional development as well as for helping fulfill the company's talent acquisition goals. Educating managers on how to use their network for employee referrals and rehires is a win for everyone.

Encourage Managers to Build a Network

On a side note, there's another reason to encourage managers to build a network, and that's for their *future* job opportunities. Before you slam the book closed because I'm suggesting helping managers find their next job, hear me out.

We are all passive job seekers today. Or we have a side hustle. Or both. The way to keep the best talent is by having a healthy workplace culture and by treating employees right. It's not by withholding information or opportunities from them.

In my first HR job, my boss taught me how to network. She took me to monthly SHRM chapter meetings and encouraged me to become a volunteer leader so I could learn how to network. Meanwhile, her boss, the chief financial officer (CFO), thought that networking was a waste. Yes, he would let us go to meetings, but he never networked with anyone.

Then one day our company was sold. And shortly after that, our new owners arrived and relieved our CFO of his responsibilities. It wasn't a mean or ugly scene. A generous package was given to the CFO. It was business. But guess what? He didn't know how to network to help land his next job.

None of us ever want to be in the position of eliminating someone's job. But if you are, wouldn't it be better knowing that the employee had the skills to find another position?

Which leads me to a conversation about employee poaching. I've spoken with many HR professionals over the years about training, and they have shared their frustrations. Not that training wasn't effective or that it cost too much. But that senior managers weren't open to training because they were afraid of developing employees . . . because those employees might leave.

They called it the "poaching factor."

Honestly, this defies all logic. It doesn't make sense that managers would say, "We don't want to train our employees. Because if we train them, they'll become smart and talented. Then some other company will steal them away from us. So we better not to do training."

Let's bust this myth once and for all.

If you don't train your employees, they will leave. Why? Because *you're not training them.* Employees want to know that the company values them and will make an investment in their professional development.

If you don't train your employees, you're making the strategic decision to develop a crappy workforce. One that will not be able to help your business succeed with increased profits and market share.

This logic about employee training applies to manager onboarding too. If companies do not train new managers to be successful, they will get frustrated and leave. Training is good for both the employee and the company. And dare I say if you train an employee, and he or she leaves . . . it's okay. My guess is the employee didn't go to training with the sole purpose of quitting afterward. Other issues could have contributed to the employee leaving, which the employee may reveal in the exit interview.

As we're talking about new managers building a network, another possibility to consider is that sometimes employees *need* to leave to expand their knowledge and experience. Then they can return a stronger contributor.

In the story about my first HR job, my boss taught me how to network. And I did leave for another job. It was a good move for my career. My boss and I stayed in touch, and years later, she contacted me about coming back to the company. Leaving an organization doesn't have to close doors. People close doors.

Companies that are concerned about the poaching factor and not training their employees are creating their self-fulfilling prophecy. When you don't train your employees, you're helping your business competition succeed.

We want employees who are able to solve their problems. How many times have we heard the phrase, "Don't just bring me a problem; bring me a solution"? We need the same for managers. They should be able to identify a problem and seek an answer. The answer doesn't always have to come from HR or their manager.

Organizations will reap greater rewards by encouraging managers to develop internal and external networks. The company doesn't have to organize a formal meeting or group. Let the managers create them based on their needs. The goal is for them to share information and become better managers. Because we want our managers to succeed. So they can get promoted again.

In the next chapter, we'll talk about onboarding managers for the role they have today while preparing them for greater responsibilities in the future with your organization.

Chapter 18.

Preparing Managers for Their Next Promotion

One of the reasons we're having this conversation about manager onboarding is because the workforce is changing. But you already know that. Millennials are the largest population in the workplace.[1] Their lives have been shaped by technology. Automation plays a huge role in the way we do business, and there are predictions that robotics will be a huge factor in the not-too-distant future.[2] Roughly one-third of the workforce holds a freelance job, whether that's to earn extra money or to maintain a flexible schedule.[3] And finally, the number of virtual workers has almost doubled in the past decade.

All of these statistics point toward change in the workplace. Change in the workplace translates into changes where jobs are concerned.[4] Organizations are going to create new jobs and redesign existing ones. And this means new roles for employees and managers. Hence, more onboarding.

That's why the conversation about creating a replacement plan and succession plan is so important. We touched on replacement and succession plans in Chapter 5, but it's worth repeating. At some point, current managers will resign, retire, or unfortunately die. (I know, it sounds morbid. But we are all mortal. People get sick. They have unfortunate accidents. And as much as we might hate to admit it, we get old. According to *The Washington Post*, 60 percent of workers ages 65 and older had full-time jobs in 2014.[5]) When managers leave, regardless of the reason, they need to be replaced, and the new manager will need onboarding.

Even if someone is currently a manager and moves into a "new" managerial role, onboarding that person needs to be a consideration. In my experience, there is a difference in responsibilities between supervisors, managers, directors, and vice presidents.

Organizations need to be constantly thinking about the future—and where they will find future talent. So it makes complete sense to be constantly developing managers for future roles. The first place to look is your existing development opportunities, which includes this onboarding program.

Mentors and Coaches

Two logical extensions to manager onboarding are mentoring programs and coaching programs. It's important to understand, though, that mentors and coaches are different and that they bring different value to the organization.

Some individuals advocate having a mentor versus a coach. I've heard the difference defined as a mentor is someone *you* pick and a coach is someone that *they* pick. I'm not sure if I completely agree that the distinction is who chooses whom, because managers can regularly coach their employees, even without a formal coaching program.

In both situations (mentoring or coaching), the individuals involved have to want to be in the relationship. Otherwise, it's a waste of organizational resources. Now, I do realize that sometimes mentoring or coaching relationships are created without much of a formal selection process. When that happens, everyone involved is given the extra task of trying to build a relationship from a position of being "assigned" instead of "selected."

My view is that the difference between mentoring and coaching is subject and process oriented.

- Mentors are typically subject matter experts in the topic they are mentoring. Their method involves teaching and development. They are passing along their knowledge and skills.
- Coaches are focused on listening, questioning, and processes. Their methods focus on action plans, goals, and accountability. They are helping someone achieve a goal that's been set.

This doesn't imply that one method is superior to another. In fact, it only heightens the importance of choosing the right one. Coaching might be best in situations when there's a skill or knowledge gap but not a clear path to address it. Mentoring may be a good option when employees are confident about what they want to do, but they need direction.

I can also see where, in certain situations, it might be helpful to have more than one mentor, depending on what a person is trying to accomplish. Not sure about multiple coaches—since they are process oriented, that situation might be confusing.

So when you go back and look at your organizational assessment (see Chapter 7), are there opportunities for coaching, mentoring, or both?

Creating a Coaching Program

When I think about coaching programs, I see two ways to approach the activity: Organizations can use outside coaches, or they can create an internal coaching program. (Oh, and there's one more way that I call "DIY." I'll save that for later in the chapter.) Each has advantages and disadvantages (see Table 18.1).

Table 18.1. Advantages and Disadvantages of Coaching

	Internal Coaches	External Coaches
Advantages	• Can be an affordable option • Because it's a company program, it can have greater consistency • Better understanding of the organization and processes • Able to respond faster and provide real-time feedback	• Often valuable for executives and in low-trust situations • Good in situations where political neutrality is necessary • Could be perceived as more objective • Might have greater expertise and experience
Disadvantages	• Role ambiguity between the coaching responsibilities and regular role • Potential challenges with confidentiality	• Often expensive • The title of executive coach isn't regulated, so results can vary widely

The direction you choose will be contingent on company resources (not only money but personnel), corporate culture, and the purpose of coaching. It's also possible that the organization might choose to have both internal and external coaches.

Before we go any further, I do want to point out something about coaching. I think there are times when coaching has received a negative reputation as an activity that's done for poor-performing managers. That's simply not true. Well, yes, organizations do use coaching as an intervention for poor-performing managers, but it's not the *only* use for coaching.

Manager coaching is an excellent tool for helping managers achieve goals and manage major change. On a personal note, I used an executive coach my first year as a consultant. The coaching helped me stay focused and work through the transition from working inside corporations to working on my own. I used a coach a few years later when my firm acquired another training company. Again, coaching allowed me the opportunity to stay focused and accountable while we were bringing this new organization into our existing company.

If you decide to go the external coach route, there are many well-known and successful coaching practices and individual coaches that can be engaged. Before you hire a coach, keep in mind these tips:

- *Make sure the coach is qualified.* Yes, there are coaching certifications, but we both know that "certified" and "qualified" are two different things. What I mean is, make sure that the coach being considered has the knowledge, skills, abilities, and experience to be successful in the assignment. Different coaching assignments require different skills and backgrounds.

- *Make sure the coach and the manager have chemistry.* I'm a firm believer that the managers being coached should have the final say in who their coach will be. They need to trust their coach and be accountable to them. Coaching is about accomplishing goals, and if the chemistry doesn't exist, it might be easy to put the blame of not achieving goals on the coach.

These same two considerations matter when you use internal coaches. Organizations can support employees becoming coaches for the organization. As I mentioned, coaching organizations exist—the International Coach Federation is one of the most popular. It offers professional development and credentialing programs. Professional coaches are bound by ethical standards. You can do an Internet search to find other coaching programs.

Organizations can identify, train, and certify coaches. You can build a program in which managers automatically receive coaching at certain times, like for the first six months in their new roles. Or you can build a program that allows managers to request a coach when they feel they would like one. Or both.

That's the beauty of coaching programs. They are incredibly flexible to meet the needs of the manager and the organization. You can use the same ADDIE model—assessment, design, development, implementation, and evaluation to create your coaching program (see Chapter 7).

I mentioned there's one other way to think about coaching. While it's certainly not ideal, it's better than nothing. I'll call it the DIY (do-it-yourself) method. Let me give you a little backstory to set this up. Years ago, I had the opportunity to hear Marshall Goldsmith speak about leadership. Dr. Goldsmith has been rated the number one executive coach globally as well as one of the top 10 most influential business leaders in the world. *Harvard Business Review* rated him as the "World's #1 Leadership Thinker."[6] He's the author of several books, including one of my favorites, *What Got You Here Won't Get You There.*[7]

One of the qualities that sets Goldsmith apart from others in the leadership space is his belief that he should "give everything away." I asked him where this belief came from, and he told me a story about growing up in a small town in Kentucky.

At one point, he was a fundraiser for the March of Dimes. He would go door-to-door asking for contributions, and when people gave him money, he was supposed to give them a loaf of bread to thank them for their donation. Over time, he discovered that he was far more effective at fundraising when he gave people the loaf of bread first. It helped him realize the importance of building a positive brand.

Goldsmith and many other leadership thinkers give away worksheets, questionnaires, and other resources that managers can use to make themselves better. For example, Goldsmith wrote "Questions That Make a Difference Every Day" that managers could use in almost a self-study format.[8] If you're trying to get a coaching program off the ground and need some resources, this might be a place to go.

Goldsmith also believes it is perfectly acceptable to modify his material. "I believe someone should only do what I say if it works for them.

Learning should be about what works for a person. We spend too much time critiquing others. It's a waste of time. Use your time to find out what works for you. If I have a model with six steps and you like five of them . . . then use five." Take advantage of these resources to put together something that managers will use.

Creating a Mentoring Program

Mentoring has one primary purpose—to pass along knowledge. The knowledge that is being passed directly aligns with the program goals, which are usually focused on three outcomes:

1. Career development.
2. Retention.
3. Employee engagement.

Mentoring isn't a short-term process. As much as we might like the term "Vulcan mind meld," that's not an effective way to pass along knowledge. Not yet at least. So, for now, organizations should pass along knowledge over time, give people the opportunity to process it, use it in the daily operation, and ask questions about it.

Also, contrary to popular stereotypes, mentoring does not have to be an older employee mentoring a younger employee. It also doesn't have to be a manager mentoring a line employee. It's about who has the information and who needs the information.

Like coaching, mentoring can be an internal activity in which employees mentor each other. Or individuals can seek external mentors. For example, a new HR manager in a one-person department might ask an external HR professional to be his or her mentor. Mentoring can also take place in groups.

SHRM Mentoring Program Toolkit

If you're not familiar with the Volunteer Leaders' Resource Center, offered by the Society for Human Resource Management (SHRM), you need to check it out.[9] As you know, SHRM has local chapter affiliates all over the United States. These local chapters have boards and regular programming for HR professionals. They also create programs similar to the ones we use every day at work.

Here is a case in point: the Northern Virginia Society for Human Resource Management (NOVA SHRM) and the Dulles SHRM chapter based in Herndon, Virginia, partnered to create a mentoring toolkit. It's 72 pages! Yes, 72 pages of mentoring approaches, processes, checklists, templates, and tools.[10]

As you're thinking about options for your program, remember you don't have to recreate the wheel. Lots of resources already exist. Take full advantage of them.

P.S. Even though this book is being published by SHRM, the organization hasn't once asked me to promote it and its resources over others. This book is about giving you the best information to create a manager onboarding program. But let me toss out two cents and say that resources like this mentoring toolkit are shining examples of the return on investment for your SHRM and local chapter membership.

Mentoring brings organizational value in its flexible approach to each organization's culture and business needs. Mentoring also doesn't have to be done in person. Technology tools can facilitate mentoring conversations.

I would strongly suggest creating metrics to support your mentoring program. Because coaching is based on achieving a goal, it could be said that the best way to measure coaching's success is by whether the person accomplished the goal. Mentoring, though, is about passing along information, so measuring success becomes trickier. Consider adding a few metrics specifically related to mentoring. Examples of measurements that can be developed include:

- *Program quality* represents outcomes such as percentage of mentors and mentees who have met at least once per month and percentage of completion in the program.
- *Participant experiences* include perceptions of value, match appropriateness, and levels of trust. This applies to both the mentee and the mentor.

- *Organizational impact* is the metrics that help the organization achieve its goals. This includes work performance, retention, and recognition.

We will be diving into metrics in the next chapter, but keep in mind that part of program design should include what metrics will be used to evaluate program effectiveness, what data will be gathered to create the metric, how often the data will be gathered, and what data points will be considered acceptable and unacceptable in evaluating the effectiveness of the program.

The beauty of mentoring programs is being able to tap into the organization's current talent to develop future talent. Luckily, as your internal talent pool is strengthened by the manager onboarding program, programs like mentoring and coaching become even stronger.

I understand that developing a formal mentoring program is a big task that you might not want to take on. If you're a small company or if you just don't want to make the investment into a formal mentoring program, consider putting together some type of DIY approach that employees can use. Teach employees how to be their own mentors.

Frankly, I wouldn't have ever considered this idea until I listened to Tim Gunn and Sophia Amoruso talk about mentors during the Massachusetts Conference for Women. Gunn is the chief creative officer at Liz Claiborne and one of the mentors on the reality television program "Project Runway." He's known for telling designers to "Make it work!" during the competition. Amoruso is the author of *#GIRLBOSS*[11] and founder of the fashion brand Nasty Gal, named one of *Inc.* magazine's fastest-growing companies in 2012.

My takeaway from their session was "be your own mentor."

That's right. Don't wait for anyone else to help you. Be tenacious and create your own success. Rely on yourself—and not on anyone else—to turn your goals into reality. It was an interesting message coming from a guy who makes his living being a mentor on television. But he and Amoruso pointed out four things about mentors that convinced me there could be some truth in their advice:[12]

- *Your mentor cannot define success for you.* So true. Everyone's version of success is different. You have to define what success looks like for you.

- *Your mentor can't want your success more than you do.* To be successful, you have to want your success more than anyone else.
- *Your mentor cannot tell you what to do.* Yes, he or she can make recommendations, but you have to do it. No one else is going to do the work.
- *Your mentor cannot make you successful.* Notice the three items we've just talked about. You have to define success, want success, and work toward success.

Gunn and Amoruso admitted that not everyone has the same opportunities in work and life. But they were both passionate about the importance of individuals taking control of their own learning—whether that's by watching a video, reading a book, or listening to a podcast. I thought the advice they offered about becoming your own mentor could be applicable for all of us at any stage in our careers:

- Give yourself permission to discover yourself.
- Do all you can with what you have.
- Get comfortable with radical ideas.

I could see these pieces of advice being something I'd want to look at on a regular basis. Especially when I think I'm stuck. They might make for great messages to share with managers in job aids, bookmarks, and other materials. I've thought about creating phone screen savers or stickers to remind myself that I'm a work in progress and that I need to make the most of the resources I have—and to be open to new and different ideas. Those aren't necessarily things I need another person for. But I do need the encouragement.

Those are things, as Gunn would say, I need to "make it work!" for myself.

Real-Time Development at PwC

In addition to creating company programs to support managers and to holding managers accountable for developing themselves, organizations have the opportunity to build cultures that allow employees and managers to support each other. At the 2015 Great Place to Work conference,

I heard about PricewaterhouseCoopers' (PwC's) real-time development program and thought it would make a great addition to a manager on-boarding effort.

PwC's onboarding programs are a portfolio of multimonth, multimodal experiences that begin with a face-to-face arrival program tailored to each type of new hire, which they refer to as a "joiner." I must admit that I like the term joiner; it acknowledges that the employee made the decision as much as the company. PwC onboards thousands of new joiners each year, with a majority of them coming into the firm as interns, campus recruits, or experienced hires.

The program begins with a three-day face-to-face arrival program designed to help new joiners feel welcomed and appreciated; understand the company's purpose, vision, and strategy; acquire technical skills specific to the company's technologies; and practice the behaviors that will help them begin developing as professionals.

The program is emceed by a certified facilitator and leadership coach The program uses a variety of instructional methods, including videos, exercises, small group activities, and mobile.

- *Day 1.* The program focuses on getting the new joiners up and running. Q&A sessions, technology "demo and do" breakouts, information tables, and networking elements provide details about navigating the company, how and where to find information, and the basics of laptop functionality and common company tools.

- *Day 2.* The facilitation team engages the new joiners through a mix of table-group and large-group dialogue. Videos, activities, and self-reflection are used to reinforce key messages and knowledge of the firm's business and strategy. New joiners simulate delivering the company experience and working in a culture of real-time development during a bike-building activity (yes, they actually build bicycles). The day concludes with a facilitated discussion encouraging new joiners to think about the value of their career.

- *Day 3.* The focus shifts to a deeper dive on the company's culture of real-time development, and the firm's behaviors and personal development, using a mix of facilitated discussion, videos, activities, and self-reflection. The program concludes on a high note with what to expect of the remaining onboarding experience, followed by a bike-building deliverable presentation to the sponsor charity (see, I told you they build bicycles).

New joiners are guided through the next phase of their onboarding experience by using an onboarding portal. It's a one-stop shop for everything new joiners need to get started, as well as support and coaching from their career coach, mentor, and local human resources. The next few months involve a mix of learning experiences in their markets, technical training, e-learn courses, and real-time development.

While PwC is committed to building leaders at all staff levels, specific components targeting management take place the managers' multimonth onboarding experience.

- Day 1: New joiners participate in a "leadership meet and greet." During this session the future leaders have the opportunity to start building their network, ask questions they have about the company, and understand the pivotal role they will play in engaging junior new joiners throughout the 3-day program. They also have a professional photographer onsite to take these leaders' professional headshots, thereby facilitating their integration into the sales and pursuit process.
- Day 2: New joiners play a key role in driving exercises related to the leadership development experience. For example, during the bike build activity, they play an enhanced role that mimics the engagement roles they will serve in after the onboarding program.

As new joiners begin their careers, leaders at all staff levels are fully immersed into the company's leadership development program. They learn about how they can develop themselves and others, and how real-time development plays a key role in the culture. Managers and above learn about their roles as a career coaches and relationship leaders. Leaders at all levels are expected to solicit and deliver regular in-the-moment feedback, delegate for development, and teach each other new things to foster a culture of continuous improvement and growth.

Real-time development (RTD) plays a key role throughout the new joiner experience and leadership development program at PwC.

New joiners have the opportunity during onboarding to further define and practice real-time development, while engaging in discussion and activities that underscore the benefits of developing every day, everywhere. This creates a work environment where new joiners commit to ways they can support and activate a culture of real-time development.

Example: Real-Time Development (RTD) Activity

Here's an example of how managers can be exposed to real-time development.

New managers pair up, with one participant being identified as the "artist," sitting with his or her back to the screen and the other participant being identified as the "coach" facing the screen.

The coach describes the image to the artist so he or she can draw it on paper, giving guidance on what to draw as well as feedback on how well the image that the artist is drawing matches the actual image on the screen.

During this activity, the artist's role is to receive coaching and real-time feedback from the coach in order to draw the correct image.

At the conclusion of the exercise the participants are asked to share their feedback on the experience.

One aspect that I thought was particularly compelling was the continuous reminders of RTD behaviors in company communications and, most importantly, in the new joiner's daily work through interactions with their teams and career coach. Real-time development has become a core part of PwC culture, and new joiners play a key role in fostering the mindset shift.

At the completion of each program, a survey is sent to all the program participants. These questions solicit feedback on the environment, course materials and design, facility, learning effectiveness, instructors, value, and specific program modules. The results of the program survey are analyzed regularly, so any corrective actions required to address scores that did not meet or exceed the program goals are implemented.

In addition, new joiners receive an onboarding survey where they provide feedback on their entire onboarding experience, starting from prehire activities through assimilation into their full-time roles. The results are reviewed by all stakeholders involved in the onboarding process, including learning and development, human resources, and recruiting teams.

Creating a Knowledge Management Infrastructure

The last area of knowledge sharing that I wanted to mention is the formal process of knowledge management (KM).[13] With coaching and mentoring, we've been talking about exchanges between individuals or groups. Knowledge management is a process focused on identifying, capturing, and distributing organizational knowledge to the people who need it.

In looking at preparing managers for the future, organizations might consider an internal process either as a replacement for or in addition to programs like mentoring or coaching. There are a couple of reasons. For instance, if the organization has a large portion of the workforce that is of retirement age, having a knowledge management infrastructure in place could make a lot of sense. The knowledge from that soon-to-be retiring worker is available to the entire company and not just to a few employees the retiring worker might have mentored or coached. The other reason is that knowledge management isn't simply a process of capturing data when people are leaving. Knowledge management can be used every day.

Again, organizations might create coaching or mentoring programs as well, but keep in mind the focus of knowledge management as an organizational process. I think this gives organizations a lot of flexibility to introduce knowledge sharing in a way that fits their culture. Depending on the findings from your ADDIE assessment, you can incorporate the pieces that work best in the order that makes the most sense. It's not an "either/or" situation but more of a "both/and."

As you are thinking about knowledge management processes, consider these questions:

- *What knowledge is important to the organization?* Companies have piles of information; the question is what's the most critical. The goal with knowledge management isn't to store everything. It's to retain the relevant parts.

- *Where is this knowledge currently stored?* Once you've identified the most essential pieces of information, then figure out where they are currently found. For example, a key piece of information the company will want to retain is about business competitors. Where is (or who has) those data right now?
- *How will that information be gathered, stored, and accessed?* The relevant information has to be brought together in some formal process. It needs to be organized in a consistent, intuitive way so people will be able to access it when necessary.

Knowledge management is an intensive project, but it brings tremendous value to the entire organization. As companies grow and expand into new markets, managers change roles, and they move to new locations. It's hard to remember who was around when this or that happened. Even if the management team remains the same, it's hard to remember all the little details about projects. Knowledge management can provide the information needed to make decisions and solve problems.

Knowledge Is Power, When We Share It

Remember that old saying, "knowledge is power," and how much we don't want it to be true because it implies someone is on a power trip? Well, knowledge is power . . . but only when we share it.

Managers need to share their knowledge around the organization. They need to pass along historical knowledge about business and customers. They need to share knowledge with employees so learning takes place. And lastly, they need to share knowledge when they are moving up the career ladder or preparing for their departure.

In this section, we've discussed some programs and processes that can be used after a formal onboarding session to help managers be successful—assessments, professional development, networking groups, coaching, and mentoring. Organizations have a wide variety of options available to create and grow their manager onboarding program.

The last section focuses on what could be the two most important components in creating a manager onboarding program—how to measure results and how to maintain it.

Part VI:

Measuring Program Effectiveness

"What gets measured gets managed."

—Peter Drucker

Chapter 19.
Measuring Program Effectiveness

At this point, the people you sold the program to back in Chapter 6 will want to know how the manager onboarding is doing. Regardless of the individual components in the manager onboarding program, it's necessary to measure results. Besides, you'll want to monitor your progress to fine-tune things along the way.

I'm a big fan of using easy-to-calculate metrics. The more complicated the metrics are, the more they are open to scrutiny. That's not to say that complex metrics lack value; but if you're not doing a metrics scorecard right now, don't make the first metrics coming from HR big, long, and complicated. Start small, get people hooked on seeing good numbers, and then add more.

Metrics That You're Probably Already Calculating

In Chapter 5, we talked about cost-per-hire. This is a metric you're probably calculating right now that could be used as an indicator of success. (Note: If you're not calculating cost-per-hire, you probably should be. It's next to impossible to budget recruiting expenses if you don't know how much it costs to hire someone.)

Logically, a manager onboarding program should positively affect cost-per-hire because the idea is that the program will better prepare managers for their roles, so they stay longer, and you don't have to hire as frequently. Or new managers are hired by referrals versus more expensive methods. Reversely, the program might not affect cost-per-hire if the organization is in a growth mode and a lot of recruiting is taking place. Once the growth phase plateaus, you should see the positive impact.

Other metrics that companies should consider tracking include yield ratios and turnover rate. Yield ratios provide a comparison of the number of applicants at one stage in the process to the number in the next stage. An example could look something like an inverse pyramid in Figure 19.1.

Figure 19.1. Yield Ratio Example

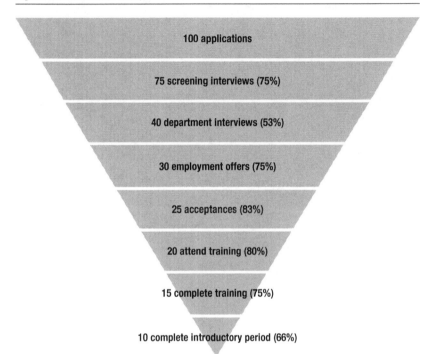

100 applications

75 screening interviews (75%)

40 department interviews (53%)

30 employment offers (75%)

25 acceptances (83%)

20 attend training (80%)

15 complete training (75%)

10 complete introductory period (66%)

In this example, the company knows that it takes 100 applicants to yield 10 new hires. But the yield ratio also tells the company that only one in three candidates complete the onboarding phase between offer letter and introductory period. The hiring team (for example, recruiters, hiring managers, trainers) can use this information to identify potential disconnects in the process.

It might also be possible to take the yield ratio one step further and calculate the ratio of employees who are still with the company after six months or one year. It's one of the aspects to yield ratios that I like;

you have some flexibility with this calculation. You could calculate yield ratios for hourly employees and another for salaried to see if there are noteworthy differences.

Lastly, turnover rate measures the rate that employees leave the organization. According to the Society for Human Resource Management (SHRM), the calculation for turnover rate is:

$$\frac{\text{Number of separations during the month}}{\text{Average number of employees during the month}} \times 100$$

The easiest way to calculate the average number of employees during the month is to take the employee count from the payroll report at the beginning and end of the month, add them together, and divide by two. Turnover rate is also flexible. It can be calculated by department, position, or job status to show the relationship between onboarding, management, and retention.

Measuring New-Manager "Orientation"

I'd like to think that, as a result of this book, many companies will create, at minimum, a new-manager orientation program. When it occurs, how long it is, and what format it takes are all subject to a company's culture. However, the orientation program is training and should have an evaluation.

In Chapter 10, I outlined Donald Kirkpatrick's four levels of evaluation. It's common to perform a Level 1 evaluation (reaction) at the end of the session. Not only does it offer some sense of how participants felt about the session, but it can include questions regarding future training that could be helpful (for example, what would you like to see in future training sessions?).

Evaluating Participant Behavior on the Job

However, we know that the real measurement of success for the manager onboarding program is going to be participant *behavior*. One way to gather data for a Level 3 evaluation (behavior) is by soliciting feedback. I remember running into a client months after conducting an onsite leadership training program. She told me that she knew the managers had enjoyed the training because they were doing what we had covered during the program. That's the behavior we're looking for.

Feedback, whether it's anecdotal or via a survey, can provide qualitative results about the onboarding process. Companies want to create a work environment where new managers feel comfortable offering feedback and suggestions for improvement. There's a wonderful window of opportunity.

New managers have fresh eyes and perspectives. But they will only have them for so long. Then they become part of the "that's the way we've always done it" crowd. This isn't to say that people will resist change or can't change. It means that, somewhere along the line, our viewpoint becomes different because we have become comfortable. When I worked in hotels, we called it "not noticing the dirt."

What's the first thing you notice when you enter a building for the first time? That's right—all the scratches, bumps, and marks. You notice the dirt. Once you start entering the building every day, well, all of those scratches become just a part of the building. Some people might even call it "charm."

The key is reaching out and soliciting feedback before those new managers grow comfortable. New managers are so excited when they start. Companies need to leverage this and come to understand how to keep that high level of enthusiasm. I've seen many occasions when a new manager is so thrilled and has tons of ideas only to become disillusioned. You know, that whole "the honeymoon's over" thing. So as you're planning to solicit feedback about the program, here are some things to consider:

- *Be sincere.* If you say you want feedback, then really want it. Otherwise, it's just lip-service, and everyone knows it. People will stop telling you what you need to know and start saying what you want to hear.
- *Identify who to ask for feedback.* Obviously, you want to get feedback from the new managers. But don't forget to solicit feedback from the new manager's boss, who should have an opinion about how the new manager is performing. Also, ask for feedback from

the trainers, coaches, mentors, or other individuals involved in the program.

- *Do something with the feedback.* The absolute worst thing you can do is ask for feedback and do nothing with it. Even if the company isn't prepared to act on it right away, let the manager know. I believe a reasonable person understands you can't do everything at the same time. What's hard to explain is not giving someone a reply.
- *Find the right time.* It's great to ask for feedback about the new-hire process on an employee's first day or ask about training during orientation. But that isn't enough. A new hire hasn't really been exposed to enough to offer valid comments. So continue to get those first impressions, but consider adding a feedback discussion at 90 days or six months.

Figure out what information you're looking for. I recently designed an onboarding program for an organization that thought employees needed to know A, B, and C on the first day. When we talked with employees, they said, "I needed to know X, Y, and Z right away. Didn't use A for weeks. No one mentioned B for months." So understanding what people need to know is good. Learning when people need to know it is even better.

Ultimately, any company that wants to improve feedback—whether it's for new managers or existing employees—needs to create and nurture an organizational culture that supports feedback. Before deciding that the focus of improving feedback lies with employees, make sure that the company's messages align with their actions.

Developing Feedback Questions

In developing a feedback survey, the company can include questions with a Likert scale response (Scale: 1 = Strongly Disagree, 2 = Disagree, 3 = Undecided, 4 = Agree, 5 = Strongly Agree) to measure responses over time. Here are a few examples:

- I felt welcome on my first day.

- The information I needed to know was provided in new manager orientation.
- I learned where to find additional information after orientation.
- The work I am doing today is the role that was explained to me during the recruitment process.

A survey like this with a scale can be completed electronically. And it could also be designed to be anonymous, which might make new managers feel a little more comfortable initially. If the surveys start to show some trends, a series of follow-up questions could be developed and asked during one-on-one interviews with new managers and their boss.

Speaking of one-on-one interviews, I once worked for an organization that put together checklists for new employees, including new managers. During orientation, employees received the checklist for their position. It listed activities that needed to be completed within the first 90 days.

After orientation, new employees and their manager (or a subject matter expert) covered items on the list. Once an item was completed, the new employees and the people who went over the activity with them signed off on the items. Employees and managers regularly met one-on-one to make sure the checklist was being completed.

Organizations could use this same idea as part of their onboarding program and as part of the evaluation process. Let's say, all new managers are given a list of 10 items they need to do within 90 days after new-manager orientation. The new managers can regularly review the list with their boss. And the company can track how many items are typically completed 30 days, 60 days, and 90 days post-orientation.

New Manager Experience: A Sample

To help you see how all the individual components of a manager onboarding program come together to deliver results, here's an example of how a program might work.

Company XYZ's New Manager Experience is an opportunity to drive a strong and consistent leadership culture and to ensure global consistency where possible. The program goals are to:

- Provide a clear path to onboarding for new managers globally
- Address an emerging need to empower front line managers and build manager capability
- Provide an easy way to find tools and resources which enable managers to execute key responsibilities
- Set expectations and build leadership mindset at the beginning of one's leadership journey

The program will allow new managers to learn through a number of different modalities (such as virtual and classroom instructor-led-training, videos, toolkits, and social networking sites). In addition, there will not be a defined end to the program as it is also the entry point into the Company XYZ leadership development program.

The program will be designed by a global working group, which includes learning and development, recruiting, compensation, employee relations, and talent and performance management. A needs assessment will be conducted by surveying and interviewing business partners to understand the company's global business needs. The program is expected to take one year to design and implement.

The program will start with a formal invitation to participate, which includes a welcome video from the CEO, a video overviewing program expectations, a 90-day checklist, a link to the company's internal collaboration site, and a link to register for a two-hour virtual instructor-led session on management essentials.

Once someone completes the management essentials session, they will receive weekly toolkits which take a deeper dive into their management role. These will be sent over a 7-week period to keep them engaged even after the formal training component is complete. New managers will continue to have access to the collaboration site and all new manager onboarding resources for as long as they are with the Company.

After six months in the manager role, participants are invited to register for the leadership development program.

Evaluations will be conducted on a regular basis. New managers will be asked to rate the effectiveness of the program, the relevance of the content, and whether they would recommend the course to others.

New manager onboarding is an important program that requires support from both HR and managers alike. New manages are craving information about their career path and they want the information sooner and through different channels. This is what new manager onboarding has to offer.

New manager onboarding also requires regular communication. In addition to participant evaluations, internal stakeholders will be asked for feedback and input. This new manager onboarding experience reinforces that new-manager onboarding is different from manager development. It takes a well-thought-out strategy and lots of communication to make it happen.

Return on Investment for the Program

In addition to evaluating the effectiveness of each component of the program, you have to measure the return on the investment (ROI), meaning you need to examine if the benefits of the program outweigh the costs. I like using these two ROI models from SHRM.[1]

Benefit Cost Ratio (BCR) = Program Benefit / Program Cost

When the BCR is greater than 1, the benefits outweigh the costs. Translation: The program is a success! When the BCR is less than 1, the costs of the program outweigh the benefits. This doesn't necessarily translate into failure, but it does mean that there should be an examination to see if changes or modifications are necessary.

The second model is a more traditional calculation for ROI:

ROI (%) = (Program Benefit - Program Cost) x 100 / Program Cost

A result greater than 100 means that a benefit is realized from the program (that is, success!) On the other hand, if the result is less than 100, it means the program is running at a loss. Again, that doesn't equate with failure, but you will have to take a close look at the program to make some adjustments.

This is also a good time to mention that, when it comes to measuring ROI, unfortunately, some things are difficult to measure. For instance, I ran across the article, "The Powerful Way Onboarding Can Encourage Authenticity."[2] It's a great read about focusing on authentic identity using socialization programs. But it raises the question, "How can I measure authenticity?"

Measurements Need to Align with Goals

Bottom line: There are ways to measure the success of the company's manager onboarding program. The key is to be selective, start small, and use the results to continuously improve.

Our final chapter is focused on the "continuously improve" part, because it would be a real shame to spend all this time, energy, and company resources creating a manager onboarding program, then have it become obsolete.

Chapter 20.

Maintaining the Program

Congratulations! You've done it. The manager onboarding program is up and running. Your metrics show that the program is an initial success. There's only one last detail you need to take care of—keeping it relevant.

Any time a program is created, there needs to be a discussion about maintaining the program. I think we all understand that keeping the program current is imperative. If you've ever seen one of these, you know exactly what I'm talking about.

Employment laws change, technology changes, and feedback from stakeholders is going to necessitate creating a process for reviewing and maintaining the program.

But here's a word of caution . . . before you break open the champagne and allow the project team to disperse (and be sure to celebrate your success), have a discussion about program maintenance. If you move too quickly to celebrate your success and adjourn, the team might feel the work is "officially done." So when the conversation about revising the program comes up, it's almost a shock.

Deep down, everyone knows the program needs to be maintained. So make it a part of the project team's responsibility to develop a maintenance plan for the manager onboarding program.

On some level, it makes sense to talk about program maintenance at the end of the program. Now that you know what the program looks like, you can put together a plan to maintain it. It could also make sense to talk about maintenance during the design process.

Think of it as two touchpoints. First, during the design process, program maintenance should be discussed in terms of whether the organization is willing both to support all elements of the program and to allocate the resources to maintain it. For example, if the manager onboarding program is going to include a coaching component, then the company needs to be willing to dedicate budget dollars regularly to maintain the program. The last thing anyone wants is to create a program only to have pieces of it go away because the resources aren't available.

Then, after discussing program maintenance during the design process, the project team needs to put a maintenance plan in place. This is the nuts and bolts of how to keep the program current. The project team needs to agree on four topics:

1. *Responsibility.* Who will be responsible for owning the program?
2. *Content.* Which content needs committee review and approval?
3. *Frequency.* How often should the program be reviewed?
4. *Process.* What is the process for reviewing the program?

Let's look at each one in some detail.

Responsibility

Chances are, the responsibility for manager onboarding is going to fall somewhere within the HR department. That just makes sense. But there are a few things to consider.

Manager onboarding needs a point person. Managers are going to have questions. There will be regular evaluations. Someone needs to be the go-to person for this program.

The people involved in designing the program do not have to be the ones who maintain it. If your organization has a learning and development function, then it is probably involved in the design and implementation of the manager onboarding program. After that, it could be someone else in human resources who becomes the point person. Do whatever makes sense for your organization.

If you don't have a formal training review process in place, the point person will need to prompt the review. Logically, if the company reviews all of its training programs every year or two, then the manager onboarding program would automatically be included in the review. But if the firm doesn't review its training programs, then the point person needs to be in a position (functionally) in which he or she has the authority to convene a group to look at the program.

Content

Speaking of authority, the person who oversees the manager onboarding program needs to be in a position to make judgment calls about content. As evaluations and feedback about the program are collected, two types of data will be gathered: minor revisions such as typos and major revisions like changing a process.

It will be important to establish what changes can be made with or without prior approvals. For instance, if a typo is discovered, can it just be changed without anyone knowing about it? The answer is usually yes. (Oh, and for those of you who are thinking there will be no typos . . . I'm forever amazed at how many times a document can go through a proofreading process and still end up with a typo. It's not intentional; it happens to the best of us.)

But then the decisions grow more complicated. What if the company does a small rebranding effort? Obviously, the materials need to be updated. Should that be done with or without review?

A change to an employment law will dictate updating as well. Should there be a review?

It's possible there will be progressive stages when it comes to content review and updates. Some changes (like typos) don't need review. Others will be reviewed by one or two people. And finally, major changes need a full committee. Initially, it might be helpful to create a job aid or decision tree to help everyone understand and remember the content review process.

Frequency

Now it's time to figure out how often your program needs to be reviewed and updated. This might cause some controversy because you've probably spent significant time putting the program together. So there might be a group of people who are ready to be done with it for a while—and especially not talk about revising it.

This isn't because they lack support for the program. It's because the program took a long time to implement. Good programs can often take a long time to implement. Now, some of the people on the development team just want to work on something else.

It makes sense to look at the program from two phases: the first year and subsequent years. During the first year, I can definitely see some discussions coming up that may raise the question, "Should we change that in the program?" After the first year, you may experience a decline in that type of discussion because you have some experience to fall back on.

It could also make sense to establish that, during the first year, the original program team will get together twice to analyze the feedback and evaluations. The group can decide if revisions need to be made. And, on a side note, it can also be a form of recognition for the group members to see the feedback. Sometimes when a project is over, the participants never get to see the outcomes. Having a couple of get-togethers during the first year could be not only productive but a nice thing to do for the team.

After the first year, I can see making changes in both the committee and the frequency of the meetings. Having fresh eyes look at the program brings value. You'll have to decide how often you want to meet. Frequency will be driven by how often the program is conducted and the feedback that has been collected.

Process

Once the group does meet, it needs to review the information that has been collected about the program. That includes evaluations, stakeholder surveys, and anecdotal feedback. The group can handle this information in a way similar to the process used in Chapter 10 with pilot programs. Some information will prompt changes. Other information might be worth monitoring until a future meeting. And lastly, some requests will not be made for various reasons.

Unlike the pilot program, in which you might know where certain suggestions or recommendations came from, it's possible you will not know who made which suggestion. This means you can't follow up with people and explain the committee's decision. What can be done is to keep a detailed record of the meeting and the decisions that were made along with the reason. Should there be any questions, the team can use the meeting report as a supporting resource.

It's also possible that, given the visibility of the program, regular updates will be sent to the program sponsor, even after the program has been implemented. The updates could include noteworthy decisions made about what is being changed in the program or suggestions not being adopted.

Which leads to a discussion about how to implement program changes. Let's say you've implemented the manager onboarding program, and a major change in the Fair Labor Standards Act takes place, which is not out of the realm of possibilities. Yes, the program will be updated for future new managers. But what about the managers who have already gone through the program? They need the new information about this major labor law change too.

Updating the program means making sure that everyone who needs the new information has it. Maintaining the manager onboarding program doesn't simply mean thinking only about *new* managers. That's the equivalent of saying that, once new employees go through orientation, they are on their own. Updates are *their* responsibility.

That being said, the committee might not be in a position to authorize a manager update session. The individual responsible for the onboarding updates will need to communicate with the appropriate colleague what changes are being made. And they have to be prepared to discuss recommendations for conveying the updates. It could be a memo, a quick video, or possibly a short training session.

Finally, the committee should plan to maintain a historical record of the manager onboarding program and how it has evolved. In Chapter 18, we talked about knowledge management. At some point, the people who created the program won't be around—they will be in new jobs, with new companies, or relaxing on a beach somewhere in their retirement. The history of the program can be valuable to future project teams.

Manager Onboarding Makes the Company Successful

Thank you for joining me on this journey to create a manager onboarding program.

Managers play such a vital role in our organizations. They help us hire talent. They train employees to be successful in their jobs. They are responsible for engagement and motivation. And they provide employee coaching so the organization can achieve its goals.

Ensuring that managers are set up for success only makes good business sense. We want to take care of the people who take care of our employees who take care of our customers.

Manager onboarding programs can be as formal and as flexible as you want them to be. Like other company programs, they're driven by culture. But a couple of things make all organizational programs successful: using a proven process to design your program, getting buy-in at every level, measuring results, and being committed to keeping the program current.

Trust me, your managers will be thrilled that the organization is making the investment. And that excitement will show in the bottom line.

Endnotes

Preface

1. See #47 at "Top HR Statistics: The Latest Stats for HR & Recruiting Pros," Glassdoor, https://www.glassdoor.com/employers/popular-topics/hr-stats.htm.

2. Matt Charney, "The State of Candidate Experience in 10 Statistics," Recruiting Daily, May 11, 2015, http://recruitingdaily.com/the-state-of-candidate-experience-in-10-statistics/.

3. Amy Adkins, "Little Change in U.S. Employee Engagement in January," Gallup, January 2016, http://www.gallup.com/poll/189071/little-change-employee-engagement-january.aspx.

Chapter 1

1. Kenneth Blanchard and Spencer Johnson, *The One Minute Manager* (New York: William Morrow, 1982).

2. "Interview: Dr. Ken Blanchard on Leadership and Management," *HR Bartender* (blog), June 9, 2015, https://www.hrbartender.com/2015/training/interview-dr-ken-blanchard-on-leadership-and-management/.

3. "The Multi-Generational Leadership Study," Workplace Trends, November 10, 2015, https://workplacetrends.com/the-multi-generational-leadership-study/.

4. Kari R. Strobel, James N. Kurtessis, Debra J. Cohen, and Alexander Alonso, *Defining HR Success: 9 Critical Competencies for HR Professionals* (Alexandria, VA: Society for Human Resource Management, 2015).

Chapter 2

1. Andrea Ledford, "Making the Everyday Easier for New NCR Employees," NCR, August 5, 2015, http://www.ncr.com/company/blogs/everyday-made-easier/making-the-everyday-easier-for-new-ncr-employee.

2. Rachel Gillett, "This Infographic Reveals the Real Ways to Hold on to New Hires," *Fast Company*, April 30, 2014, http://www.fastcompany.com/3029820/work-smart/infographic-the-real-ways-to-hold-on-to-new-hires.

3. Stacey Harris and Erin Spencer, "2015-2016 HR Systems Survey White Paper, 18th Annual Edition," Sierra-Cedar, http://www.sierra-cedar.com/research/publications/#toggle-id-1.

4. Carina Wytiaz, "Which Is Right for Your Organization: Onboarding or Inboarding?" *a magazine*, March 2, 2015, http://blog.octanner.com/talent-management-2/which-is-right-for-your-organization-onboarding-or-inboarding.

5. See the video "The X-Model of Employee Engagement," BlessingWhite, http://blessingwhite.com/video/2012/03/12/the-x-model-of-employee-engagement/.

6. Sarah Fister Gale, "Onboarding's a Big Problem for Small Businesses," *Workforce*, July 28, 2015, http://www.workforce.com/articles/21485-onboardings-a-big-problem-for-small-businesses.

7. Talya N. Bauer, *Onboarding New Employees: Maximizing Success* (Effective Practice Guidelines Series), SHRM Foundation, 2010, http://www.shrm.org/about/foundation/products/Documents/Onboarding%20EPG-%20FINAL.pdf.

Chapter 3

1. Peter Block, *Flawless Consulting: A Guide to Getting Your Expertise Used*, 3rd ed. (San Francisco: Pfeiffer, 2011). Whether you're an internal business partner or external consultant, *Flawless Consulting* should be on every HR professional's bookshelf. We regularly talk about HR having the proverbial "seat at the table." One of the ways you get there is by adopting a consulting approach to solving organizational problems.

2. Sharlyn Lauby, "#ASTD2011: How Sears Optical Reinvented Its Corporate Culture," *SmartBlog on Leadership* (blog), June 24, 2011, http://smartblogs.com/leadership/2011/06/24/astd2011-how-sears-optical-reinvented-its-corporate-culture/.

3. Society for Human Resource Management, "Metrics Calculators," http://www.shrm.org/templatestools/samples/metrics/pages/default.aspx.

4. Jac Fitz-enz and Barbara Davison, *How to Measure Human Resource Management*, 3rd ed. (New York: McGraw-Hill, 2002).

5. Laurence Capron and Will Mitchell, *Build, Borrow, or Buy: Solving the Growth Dilemma* (Boston: Harvard Business Review Press, 2012).

Chapter 4

1. See Douglas McGregor, *The Human Side of Enterprise*, annotated edition (New York: McGraw-Hill Education, 2006).

2. "Don't Let Workplace Stress Ruin Your Labor Day Holiday," American Psychological Association, http://www.apa.org/helpcenter/labor-day.aspx.

3. Josh Bersin et al (eds.), "Global Human Capital Trends 2015: Leading in the New World of Work," Deloitte University Press, http://www2.deloitte.com/content/dam/Deloitte/na/Documents/human-capital/na_DUP_GlobalHumanCapitalTrends2015.pdf.

4. *2012 Allied Workforce Mobility Survey: Onboarding and Retention*, Allied HR IQ, http://hriq.allied.com/pdfs/AlliedWorkforceMobilitySurvey.pdf.

5. The Paperless Project website is at http://www.thepaperlessproject.com.

Chapter 5

1. Joyce O'Donnell Maroney (ed.), *Creating the Workforce—and Results—You Seek* (Chelmsford, MA: Kronos Incorporated, 2010).

2. "Baby Boomers Retire," Pew Research Center, December 29, 2010, http://www.pewresearch.org/daily-number/baby-boomers-retire/.

3. *State of Succession Planning: Are You Doing Enough to Identify and Develop Talent to Build Bench Strength?* Halogen Software, 2015, http://www.halogensoftware.com/learn/whitepapers-and-ebooks/the-state-of-succession-planning-are-you-doing-enough-to-identify-and-develop-talent-to-build-bench-strength.

4. Robin Erickson, "Benchmarking Talent Acquisition: Increasing Spend, Cost Per Hire, and Time to Fill," Bersin by Deloitte, April 23, 2015, http://www.bersin.com/blog/post/Benchmarking-Talent-Acquisition-Increasing-Spend2c-Cost-Per-Hire2c-and-Time-to-Fill.aspx.

5. *Cost-Per-Hire: American National Standard*, American National Standards, Inc. and the Society for Human Resource Management, February 8, 2012, http://www.shrm.org/TemplatesTools/HRStandards/Documents/11-0096%20HR%20Standards%20Booklet_WEB_revised.pdf.

6. Vineet Nayar, "Who Is the New CEO?," *Harvard Business Review*, July 6, 2010, https://hbr.org/2010/07/who-is-the-new-ceo/.

7. Sharlyn Lauby, "The Business Case for Managing Ourselves," *HR Bartender* (blog), August 29, 2010, https://www.hrbartender.com/2010/training/the-business-case-for-managing-ourselves/.

8. See Sharlyn Lauby, "Using Talent Pools to Develop Future Leaders," *Talent Space Blog*, March 3, 2015, http://www.halogensoftware.com/blog/using-talent-pools-to-develop-future-leaders; Sharlyn Lauby, "Should You Tell Employees They're Part of the Succession Plan?" April 1, 2014, *TalentSpace Blog*, http://www.halogensoftware.com/blog/should-you-tell-employees-theyre-part-of-the-succession-plan; and Sharlyn Lauby, "Before You Start Succession Planning . . . Do This," *TalentSpace Blog*, April 22, 2015, http://www.halogensoftware.com/blog/before-you-start-succession-planning-do-this.

Chapter 6

1. Author Interview, "Dr. John Kotter on Creating Organizational Change, *HR Bartender* (blog), November 13, 2011, https://www.hrbartender.com/2011/business-and-customers/interview-dr-john-kotter-on-creating-organizational-change/.

2. John Kotter and Holger Rathgeber, *Our Iceberg Is Melting: Changing and Succeeding under Any Conditions* (New York: St. Martin's Press, 2006).

3. John P. Kotter, *A Sense of Urgency* (Boston: Harvard Business Press, 2008).

4. Jac Fitz-enz and Barbara Davison, *How to Measure Human Resource Management*, 3rd ed. (New York: McGraw-Hill, 2002).

5. "SHRM Leading Indicators of National Employment® (LINE®)," Society for Human Resource Management, http://www.shrm.org/research/monthlyemploymentindices/line/pages/default.aspx.

6. Sharlyn Lauby, "Here's What Happens When You Kill the Performance Appraisal," *HR Bartender* (blog), June 16, 2014, https://www.hrbartender.com/2014/recruiting/heres-what-happens-when-you-kill-the-performance-appraisal.

7. Samuel A. Culbert with Lawrence Rout, *Get Rid of the Performance Review!: How Companies Can Stop Intimidating, Start Managing—and Focus on What Really Matters* (New York: Business Plus, 2010).

8.   Sharlyn Lauby, "The 7 Kinds of Power You Can use At Work," *HR Bartender* (blog), December 22, 2013, https://www.hrbartender.com/2013/recruiting/the-7-kinds-of-power-you-can-use-at-work/.

9.   One book to help develop your business acumen competency is Regan W. Garey, *Business Literacy Survival Guide for HR Professionals* (Alexandria, VA: Society for Human Resource Management, 2011).

10. Joyce Maroney, "The Scientific Method Isn't Just for Scientists," Workforce Institute at Kronos, March 14, 2014, http://www.workforceinstitute.org/blog/scientific-method-isnt-just-scientists/.

Chapter 7

1.   Deborah Tobey, *Needs Assessment Basics* (Alexandria, VA: ASTD, 2006).

2.   For a deeper dive into SAM, see this resource: Michael Allen with Richard Sites, *Leaving Addie for Sam: An Agile Model for Developing the Best Learning Experiences* (Alexandria, VA: ASTD Press, 2012).

3.   For more about the appreciative inquiry, see Diana Whitney and Amanda Trosten-Bloom, *The Power of Appreciative Inquiry: A Practical Guide to Positive Change*, 2nd ed. (San Francisco: Berrett-Koehler Publishers, 2010).

Chapter 8

1.   Sharlyn Lauby, "How to Write the Perfect Learning Objective," *OpenSesame* (blog), October 7, 2013, https://www.opensesame.com/blog/how-write-perfect-learning-objective.

2.   For details, see "Relationship Centered Learning," Brandon Hall Group, http://go.brandonhall.com/relationship_centered_learning_2012.

3.   Charles I. Levine, "On-the-Job Training," American Society for Training & Development, August 1997.

4.   Stephanie Bevegni, "Onboarding in a Box: Your Complete New Hire Resource Kit," LinkedIn *Talent Blog*, June 9, 2015, https://business.linkedin.com/talent-solutions/blog/2015/06/onboarding-in-a-box-your-complete-new-hire-resource.

5.   "Social Recruiting Survey, 2014," Jobvite, https://www.jobvite.com/wp-content/uploads/2014/10/Jobvite_SocialRecruiting_Survey2014.pdf.

6.   For additional information, see Jane Bozarth, *Social Media for Trainers: Techniques for Enhancing and Extending Learning* (San Francisco: Pfeiffer, 2010).

7.   Megan Scudellari, "The Science Myths that Will Not Die," *Nature*, December 17, 2015, 528 no. 7582, 322-325, http://www.nature.com/news/the-science-myths-that-will-not-die-1.19022.

Chapter 9

1.   I like an app called Trello, which is available for iOS and Android. It has in-app purchases, so you can decide what works with your budget.

2.   Sharlyn Lauby, "Debriefs: An Essential Skill for Teams," *HR Bartender* (blog), November 3, 2013, https://www.hrbartender.com/2013/training/debriefs-an-essential-skill-for-teams/.

3.   Scott I. Tannenbaum and Christopher P. Cerasoli, "Do Team and Individual Debriefs Enhance Performance? A Meta-Analysis," *Human Factors*, 55(1), February 2013, 231-245, http://hfs.sagepub.com/content/55/1/231.full.pdf +html; also see Lauby, "Debriefs: An Essential Skill for Teams."

Chapter 10

1.   Michael Wilkinson, *The Secrets of Facilitation: The SMART Guide to Getting Results with Groups*, 2nd ed. (San Francisco: Jossey-Bass, 2012).

2.   Suzanne Ghais, *Extreme Facilitation: Guiding Groups through Controversy and Complexity* (San Francisco: Jossey-Bass, 2005).

3.   Val Gee and Sarah Gee, *Business Improv: Experiential Learning Exercises to Train Employees to Handle Every Situation with Success* (New York: McGraw-Hill Education, 2011).

4.   See "The Kirkpatrick Model," Kirkpatrick Partners, http://www.kirkpatrickpartners.com/OurPhilosophy/TheKirkpatrickModel/tabid/302/Default.aspx.

Chapter 12

1.   Norman Maclean, *Young Men and Fire* (University of Chicago Press, 1992).

2.   Don Tapscott and Art Caston, *Paradigm Shift: The New Promise of Information Technology* (New York: McGraw-Hill, 1992).

3.   "Number of Monthly Active Twitter Users Worldwide from 1st Quarter 2010 to 3rd Quarter 2015 (in Millions)," Statista, 2016, http://www.statista.com/statistics/282087/number-of-monthly-active-twitter-users/.

4. Kristin Piombino, "Infographic: 67% of People Are More Likely to Buy from Brands They Follow on Twitter," ragan.com, January 15, 2014, http://www.ra-gan.com/Main/Articles/Infographic_67_of_people_are_more_likely_to_buy_fr_47802.aspx.

5. Larry Bossidy and Ram Charan, *Execution: The Discipline of Getting Things Done* (New York: Crown Business, 2002).

6. For a deeper discussion of Gantt charts and PERT charts, see "Gantt Charts: Planning and Scheduling Team Projects," MindTools, https://www.mindtools.com/pages/article/newPPM_03.htm and "Critical Path Analysis and PERT Charts: Planning and Scheduling More Complex Projects," MindTools, https://www.mindtools.com/critpath.html.

Chapter 13

1. For a discussion about soft skills relative to a younger workforce, see Bruce Tulgan, *Bridging the Soft Skills Gap: How to Teach the Missing Basics to Todays Young Talent* (San Francisco: Jossey-Bass, 2015).

2. "It Takes More than a Major: Employer Priorities for College Learning and Student Success: Overview and Key Findings," Association of American Colleges & Universities and Hart Research Associates, 2013, https://www.aacu.org/leap/presidentstrust/compact/2013SurveySummary.

3. "SMB Communications Pain Study White Paper: Uncovering the Hidden Cost of Communications Barriers and Latency," SIS International Research, https://www.sisinternational.com/smb-communications-pain-study-white-paper-un-covering-the-hidden-cost-of-communications-barriers-and-latency/.

4. For example, McGraw-Hill (www.mhprofessional.com) publishes the Perfect Phrases series.

5. Travis Bradberry, "Why You Need Emotional Intelligence to Succeed," *Inc.*, March, 12, 2015, http://www.inc.com/travis-bradberry/why-you-need-emo-tional-intelligence-to-succeed.html.

6. Travis Bradberry, "Why You Need Emotional Intelligence to Succeed," TalentSmart, http://www.talentsmart.com/articles/Why-You-Need-Emotional-Intelligence-To-Succeed-389993854-p-1.html.

7. To download a copy of the *Executive Playbook* e-book, go to https://business.linkedin.com/marketing-solutions/c/14/7/executive-playbook-lms.

8.   Kari R. Strobel, James N. Kurtessis, Debra J. Cohen, and Alexander Alonso, *Defining HR Success: 9 Critical Competencies for HR Professionals* (Alexandria, VA: Society for Human Resource Management, 2015), 59.

9.   Keith Ferrazzi and Tahl Raz, *Never Eat Alone: And Other Secrets to Success, One Relationship at a Time*, expanded and updated edition (New York: Crown Business, 2014).

10.   Team Gwava, "How Much Data Is Created on the Internet Each Day?" Gwava. com, November 5, 2015, https://www.gwava.com/blog/internet-data-created-daily.

Chapter 14

1.   "Little Change in U.S. Employee Engagement in January," Gallup, January 2016, http://www.gallup.com/poll/189071/little-change-employee-engagement-january.aspx; "State of the American Workplace: Employee Engagement Insights for U.S. Business Leaders," Gallup, 2013, http://www.gallup.com/services/176708/state-american-workplace.aspx. Also see, Josh Bersin, "Why Companies Fail to Engage Today's Workforce: The Overwhelmed Employee," *Forbes*, March 15, 2014, http://www.forbes.com/sites/joshbersin/2014/03/15/why-companies-fail-to-engage-todays-workforce-the-overwhelmed-employee/#1cef7e1c2b94; Robyn Reilly, "Five Ways to Improve Employee Engagement Now," Gallup, January 7, 2014, http://www.gallup.com/businessjournal/166667/five-ways-improve-employee-engagement.aspx.

2.   "SHRM Survey Findings: Financial Wellness in the Workplace," Society for Human Resource Management, May 14, 2014, http://www.shrm.org/research/surveyfindings/articles/pages/2014-financial-wellness.aspx.

3.   "Not Enough Sleep Will Decrease Productivity at Work and School," *Bolivar (MO) Herald Free Press*, October 11, 2014, http://bolivarmonews.com/neighbors/not-enough-sleep-will-decrease-productivity-at-work-and-school/article_0cc97e08-509a-11e4-8f94-5ffe07cf298f.html.

4.   J.C. Coulson, J. McKenna, and M. Field, "Exercising at Work and Self-Reported Work Performance," *International Journal of Workplace Health Management*, 1(3), September 2008, 176-197.

5.   Caroline Cooke, "Shift Work & Absenteeism: The Bottom Line Killer," Circadian, October 14, 2014, http://www.circadian.com/blog/item/43-shift-work-absenteeism-the-bottom-line-killer.html.

6. Michael Jordan, "Failure" commercial by Nike https://www.youtube.com/watch?v=GuXZFQKKF7A.

7. Daniel Goleman, *Emotional Intelligence: Why It Can Matter More Than IQ* (New York: Bantam, 2006); for the interview, see Sharlyn Lauby, "INTERVIEW: Dr. Daniel Goleman on Staying Focused," *HR Bartender* (blog), February 5, 2014, https://www.hrbartender.com/2014/training/interview-dr-daniel-goleman-on-staying-focused/.

8. Sharlyn Lauby, "Future Leaders Need Organizational Mindfulness," *HR Bartender* (blog), May 17, 2015, https://www.hrbartender.com/2015/training/future-leaders-need-organizational-mindfulness/.

9. See Mihaly Csikszentmihalyi, "Flow, the Secret to Happiness," TED Talks, Feb. 2004, http://www.ted.com/talks/mihaly_csikszentmihalyi_on_flow.

10. Sharlyn Lauby, "Want More Employee Productivity? Figure Out Their 'Flow'," *HR Bartender* (blog), May 17, 2015, https://www.hrbartender.com/2015/training/want-more-employee-productivity-figure-out-their-flow/.

Chapter 15

1. For example, see James J. McDonald, Jr., *California Employment Law: An Employer's Guide* (Alexandria, VA: Society for Human Resource Management, 2016).

2. A couple of resources written for the non-lawyer manager are Max Muller, *The Manager's Guide to HR: Hiring, Firing, Performance Evaluations, Documentation, Benefits, and Everything Else You Need to Know*, 2nd edition (New York: AMACOM and Alexandria, VA: Society for Human Resource Management, 2013) and Lisa Guerin and Amy DelPo, *The Essential Guide to Federal Employment Laws*, 5th Edition (Berkeley, CA: Nolo, 2016).

Chapter 17

1. Katharine Robinson, "Are You Unlocking the Full Potential of LinkedIn Groups?" *Undercover Recruiter* (blog), http://theundercoverrecruiter.com/unlocking-linkedin-groups/.

2. "Employee Referrals Are Gold," *China Gorman* (blog), January 19, 2016, http://chinagorman.com/2016/01/19/employee-referrals-are-gold/.

3. Stephen Burks, Bo Cowgill, Mitchell Hoffman, and Michael Housman, "The Value of Hiring through Employee Referrals," *Quarterly Journal of Economics*, May 2015, 130 no. 2, 805-839.

4. John Sullivan, "Top Performers: Here's Why Their Employee Referrals are Golden,"TLNT, May 10, 2013, http://www.eremedia.com/tlnt/top-performers-heres-why-their-employee-referrals-are-golden/.

5. Recruitment Marketing Effectiveness: Meaningful Metrics Straight from the Source, SilkRoad, http://hr1.silkroad.com/Recruitment-Marketing-Effectiveness-Registration.

6. Gerry Crispin and Mark Mehler, *Sources of Hire: Perception Is Reality*, CareerXRoads, 2013, http://careerxroads.com/news/SourcesOfHire2013.pdf; the 2014 report can be found at http://careerxroads.com/news/2014_SourceOfHire.pdf; the 2015 report can be found at http://www.slideshare.net/gerrycrispin/2015-careerxroads-source-of-hire-report-56847680.

Chapter 18

1. *15 Economic Facts about Millennials*, The Council of Economic Advisers, October 2014, https://www.whitehouse.gov/sites/default/files/docs/millennials_report.pdf.

2. Patrick Thibodeau, "Robotics, Automation Play a Big Role in Gartner's Top 10 Predictions," *Computerworld*, October 6, 2015, http://www.computerworld.com/article/2989830/it-careers/machines-are-replacing-writers-gartner-says.html.

3. Emmie Martin, "The 55 Best Companies for Freelancers," *Business Insider*, September 15, 2014, http://www.businessinsider.com/best-companies-for-free-lancers-2014-9.

4. James O'Brien, "5 Ways the Workforce Will Change in 5 Years," *Mashable*, August 25, 2014, http://mashable.com/2014/08/25/workforce-in-5-years.

5. Jonnelle Marte, "The Anti-retirement Plan: Working 9-to-5 Past 65," *Washington Post*, October 3, 2014, https://www.washingtonpost.com/news/get-there/wp/2014/10/03/the-anti-retirement-plan-working-9-to-5-past-65/.

6. "Marshall Goldsmith," Marshall Goldsmith Library, http://www.marshallgoldsmithlibrary.com/html/marshall/Marshall-Goldsmith.html.

7. Marshall Goldsmith with Mark Reiter, *What Got You Here Won't Get You There: How Successful People Become Even More Successful* (New York: Hachette Books, 2007).

8. Marshall Goldsmith, "Questions That Make a Difference Every Day," July 2006, http://www.marshallgoldsmithlibrary.com/docs/Talent-Management/Questions-Make-Difference-TM.doc.

9. Volunteer Leaders' Resource Center, Society for Human Resource Management, http://www.shrm.org/communities/volunteerresources/pages/default.aspx.

10. *Mentoring Program Toolkit: Establishing a Mentoring Program in Your Local SHRM Chapter*, NOVA/Dulles SHRM, April 2012, http://www.shrm.org/communities/volunteerresources/documents/324va_nova_dulles_mentoring_program_toolkit_april2012.pdf.

11. Sophia Amoruso, *#GIRLBOSS* (New York: Portfolio, 2014).

12. See Tim Gunn and Sophia Amoruso at the 2015 MA Conference for Women, December 10, 2015, https://www.youtube.com/watch?v=3vgWNJPKWyQ.

13. Amy Newman, "InfoLine Issue 9903: Knowledge Management," ASTD Publishing, 2002.

Chapter 19

1. Karen Kaminski and Tobin Lopes, "Return on Investment: Training and Development," Society for Human Resource Management, 2009, http://www.shrm.org/Education/hreducation/Documents/09-0168%20Kaminski%20ROI%20TnD%20IM_FINAL.pdf; also see Jack J. Phillips and Patricia Pulliam Phillips, *Proving the Value of HR: How and Why to Measure ROI*, 2d edition (Alexandria, VA: Society for Human Resource Management, 2012).

2. Dan Cable, Francesca Gino, and Bradley Staats, "The Powerful Way Onboarding Can Encourage Authenticity," *Harvard Business Review*, November 26, 2015, https://hbr.org/2015/11/the-powerful-way-onboarding-can-encourage-authenticity.

Index

M

About the Author

Sharlyn Lauby, SHRM-SCP, is the author of the HR Bartender blog and president of ITM Group Inc., a South Florida-based training and human resource consulting firm focused on helping companies retain and engage talent.

Before starting ITM Group, she was vice president of human resources for Right Management Consultants, one of the world's largest organizational consulting firms. She has designed and implemented highly successful programs for employee retention, internal and external customer satisfaction, and leadership development. Media outlets and publications such as Reuters, the *New York Times*, ABC News, the "Today" show, *Readers Digest*, *Men's Health*, Mashable, and the *Wall Street Journal* have sought out her expertise on topics related to human resources and the workplace.

She launched *HR Bartender* to provide a "friendly place for everyday workplace issues." *HR Bartender* has been recognized as one of the Top 5 Business Blogs Read by HR Professionals by SHRM and a Top 25 Must-Read Blog for Employers.

Lauby believes strongly in giving to the community. She served by appointment from former Governor Jeb Bush on the Governor's Alliance for the Employment of Citizens with Disabilities. She also served as co-lead of SHRM's Ethics and Corporate Social Responsibility special expertise panel and previously as president of HR Florida, the statewide SHRM affiliate.

Additional
SHRM-Published Books

101 Sample Write-Ups for Documenting Employee Performance Problems:
A Guide to Progressive Discipline & Termination, Second Edition
Paul Falcone

Defining HR Success: 9 Critical Competencies for HR Professionals
Kari R. Strobel, James N. Kurtessis, Debra J. Cohen, and Alexander Alonso

Destination Innovation: HR's Role in Charting the Course
Patricia M. Buhler

The EQ Interview: Finding Employees with High Emotional Intelligence
Adele B. Lynn

The Manager's Guide to HR: Hiring, Firing, Performance Evaluations,
Documentation, Benefits, and Everything Else You Need to Know, 2nd
edition
Max Muller

The Power of Stay Interviews for Engagement and Retention
Richard P. Finnegan

Stop Bullying at Work: Strategies and Tools for HR, Legal, & Risk Management
Professionals, 2nd Edition
Teresa A. Daniel and Gary S. Metcalf

Up, Down, and Sideways: High-Impact Verbal Communication for HR
Professionals
Patricia M. Buhler and Joel D. Worden